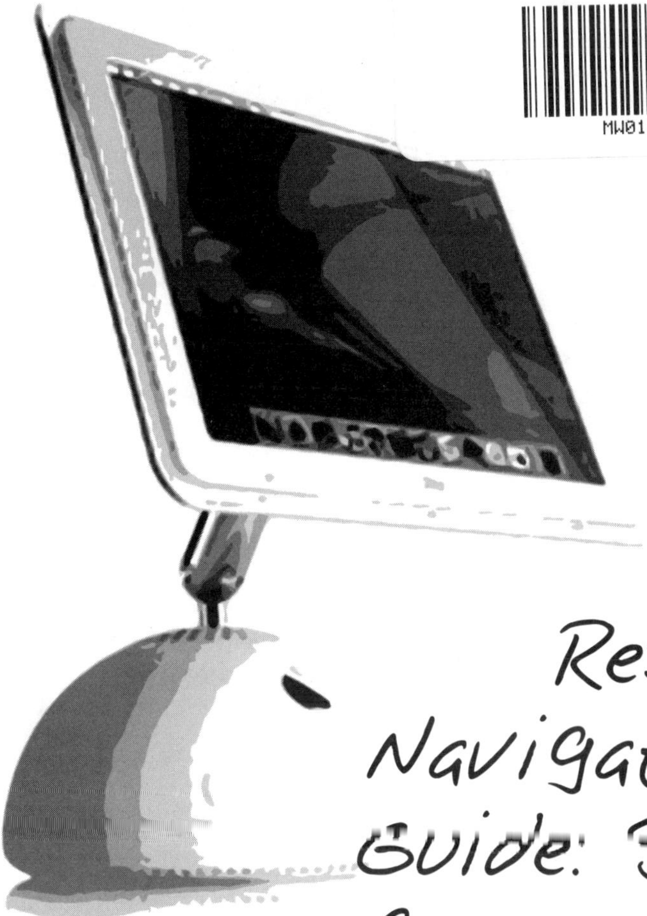

Research Navigator.com Guide: Speech Communication

Steven L. Epstein

Suffolk County Community College

Linda R. Barr

University of the Virgin Islands

PEARSON

Boston | New York | San Francisco
Mexico City | Montreal | Toronto | London | Madrid | Munich | Paris
Hong Kong | Singapore | Tokyo | Cape Town | Sydney

ISBN   0-205-51714-5

Printed in the United States of America

10 9 8 7 6 5 4 3 2   11 10 09 08

Contents

Introduction

Your professor assigns a ten-page research paper that's due in two weeks—and you need to make sure you have up-to-date, credible information. Where do you begin? Today, the easiest answer is the Internet—because it can be so convenient and there is so much information out there. But therein lies part of the problem. How do you know if the information is reliable and from a trustworthy source?

ResearchNavigator.com Guide is designed to help you select and evaluate research from the Web to help you find the best and most credible information you can. Throughout this guide, you'll find:

- **A practical and to-the-point discussion of search engines.** Find out which search engines are likely to get you the information you want and how to phrase your searches for the most effective results.
- **Detailed information on evaluating online sources.** Locate credible information on the Web and get tips for thinking critically about Web sites.
- **Citation guidelines for Web resources.** Learn the proper citation guidelines for Web sites, email messages, listservs, and more.
- **ResearchNavigator.com Guide.** All you need to know to get started with ResearchNavigator.com, a research database that gives you immediate access to hundreds of scholarly journals and other popular publications, such as *Scientific American, U.S. News & World Report,* and many others.

So before running straight to your browser, take the time to read through this copy of *ResearchNavigator.com Guide* and use it as a reference for all of your Web research needs.

P A R T 1

Research
Navigator.com

What Is ResearchNavigator.com?

ResearchNavigator.com is the easiest way for you to start a research assignment or research paper. Complete with extensive help on the research process and four exclusive databases of credible and reliable source material (including EBSCO's ContentSelect™ Academic Journal and Abstract Database, *New York Times* Search by Subject Archive, Link Library, and the *Financial Times* Article Archive), ResearchNavigator.com helps you quickly and efficiently make the most of your research time.

ResearchNavigator.com includes four databases of dependable source material to get your research process started:

1. EBSCO's ContentSelect™ Academic Journal and Abstract Database, organized by subject, contains 50–100 of the leading academic journals per discipline. Instructors and students can search the online journals by keyword, topic, or multiple topics. Articles include abstract and citation information and can be cut, pasted, emailed, or saved for later use.
2. The *New York Times* Search by Subject Archive is organized by academic subject and searchable by keyword, or multiple keywords. Instructors and students can view full-text articles from the world's leading journalists from *The New York Times*. The *New York Times* Search by Subject Archive is available exclusively to instructors and students through ResearchNavigator.com.

3. Link Library, organized by subject, offers editorially selected "Best of the Web" sites. Link libraries are continually scanned and kept up to date, providing the most relevant and accurate links for research assignments.
4. The *Financial Times* Article Archive and Company Financials provides a searchable one-year archive and five-year financials for the 500 largest U.S. companies (by gross revenue).

In addition, ResearchNavigator.com includes extensive online content detailing the steps in the research process including:

- Understanding the Research Process
- Finding Sources for your Assignment
- Using your Library for Research, with library guides to 31 core disciplines. Each library guide includes an overview of major databases and online journals, key associations and newsgroups, and suggestions for further research.
- Writing Your Research Assignment
- Finishing with Endnotes and a Bibliography

Registering with ResearchNavigator.com

http://www.researchnavigator.com

ResearchNavigator.com is simple to use and easy to navigate. The goal of ResearchNavigator.com is to help you complete research assignments or research papers quickly and efficiently. The site is organized around the following five tabs:

- The Research Process
- Finding Sources
- Using Your Library
- Start Writing
- Endnotes & Bibliography

In order to begin using ResearchNavigator.com, you must first register using the personal access code that appears in the front cover of this book.

To Register:
4. Go to **http://www.researchnavigator.com**
5. Click "Register" under "New Users" on the left side of the screen.
6. Enter the access code exactly as it appears on the inside front cover of this book. (Note: Access codes can only be used once to com-

plete one registration. If you purchased a used guide, the access code may not work. Please go to **www.researchnavigator.com** for information on how to obtain a new access code.)

7. Follow the instructions on screen to complete your registration—you may click the Help button at any time if you are unsure how to respond.

8. Once you have successfully completed registration, write down the Login Name and Password you just created and keep it in a safe place. You will need to enter it each time you want to revisit ResearchNavigator.com.

9. Once you register, you have access to all the resources in ResearchNavigator.com for twelve months.

Getting Started

From the ResearchNavigator.com homepage, you have easy access to all of the site's main features, including a quick route to four exclusive databases of source content that will be discussed in greater detail on the following pages. If you are new to the research process, you may want to start by clicking the *Research Process* tab, located in the upper right hand section of the page. Here you will find extensive help on all aspects of the research process, including:

- Overview of the Research Process
- Understanding a Research Assignment
- Finding a Topic
- Creating Effective Notes
- Research Paper Paradigms
- Understanding and Finding "Source" Material
- Understanding and Avoiding Plagiarism
- Summary of the Research Process

For those of you who are already familiar with the research process, you already know that the first step in completing a research assignment or research paper is to select a topic. (In some cases, your instructor may assign you a topic.) According to James D. Lester in *Writing Research Papers,* choosing a topic for the research paper can be easy (any topic will serve) yet very complicated (an informed choice is critical). He suggests selecting a person, a person's work, or a specific issue to study—President George W. Bush, John Steinbeck's *Of Mice and Men,* or learned dexterity with Nintendo games. Try to select a topic that will meet three demands.

1. It must examine a significant issue.
2. It must address a knowledgeable reader and carry that reader to another level of knowledge.

3. It must have a serious purpose, one that demands analysis of the issues, argues from a position, and explains complex details.

You can find more tips from Lester in the *Research Process* section of ResearchNavigator.com.

ResearchNavigator.com simplifies your research efforts by giving you a convenient launching pad for gathering data on your topic. The site has aggregated four distinct types of source material commonly used in research assignments: academic journals (Content-Select™); newspaper articles (*New York Times*), World Wide Web sites (Link Library), and international news and business data (*Financial Times*).

EBSCO's ContentSelect Academic Journal and Abstract Database

EBSCO's ContentSelect Academic Journal and Abstract Database contains scholarly, peer-reviewed journals (like the *Journal of Clinical Psychology* or the *Journal of Anthropology*). A scholarly journal is an edited collection of articles written by various authors and is published several times per year. All the issues published in one calendar year comprise a volume of that journal. For example, the *American Sociological Review* published volume 65 in the year 2000. This official journal of the American Sociological Association is published six times a year, so issues 1–6 in volume 65 are the individual issues for that year. Each issue contains between 4 and 8 articles written by a variety of authors. Additionally, journal issues may contain letters from the editor, book reviews, and comments from authors. Each issue of a journal does not necessarily revolve around a common theme. In fact, most issues contain articles on many different topics.

Scholarly journals, are similar to magazines in that they are published several times per year and contain a variety of articles in each issue, however, they are NOT magazines. What sets them apart from popular magazines like *Newsweek* or *Science News* is that the content of each issue is peer-reviewed. This means that each journal has, in addition to an editor and editorial staff, a pool of reviewers. Rather than a staff of writers who write something on assignment, journals accept submissions from academic researchers all over the world. The editor relies on these peer reviewers both to evaluate the articles, which are submitted, and to decide if they should be accepted for publication. These published articles provide you with a specialized knowledge and information about your research topic. Academic journal articles adhere to strict scientific guidelines for methodology and theoretical grounding. The information obtained in these individual articles is more scientific than information you would find in a popular magazine, newspaper article, or on a Web page.

Using ContentSelect

Searching for articles in ContentSelect is easy! Here are some instructions and search tips to help you find articles for your research paper.

Select a Database

ContentSelect's homepage features a list of databases. To search within a single database, click the name of the database. To search in more than one database, hold down the alt or command key while clicking on the name of the database.

Basic Search.   After selecting one or more databases, you must enter a keyword or keywords, then click on "go." This will take you to the basic search window. If you've selected a precise and distinctive keyword, your search may be done. But if you have too many results—which is often the case—you need to narrow your search.

Standard Search (Boolean).
- **AND** combines search terms so that each result contains all of the terms. For example, search **education AND technology** to find only articles that contain both terms.
- **OR** combines search terms so that each result contains at least one of the terms. For example, search **education OR technology** to find results that contain either term.
- **NOT** excludes terms so that each result does not contain the term that follows the "not" operator. For example, search **education NOT technology** to find results that contain the term education but not the term technology.

Search by Article Number.   Each and every article in the EBSCO ContentSelect Academic Journal and Abstract Database is assigned its own unique article number. In some cases, you may know the exact article number for the journal article you'd like to retrieve. Perhaps you noted it during a prior research session on ResearchNavigator.com. Such article numbers might also be found on a companion web site for your text, or in the text itself.

To retrieve a specific article, simply type that article number in the "Search by Article Number" field and click the **GO** button.

Advanced Search.   On the tabbed tool bar, click **Advanced Search.** The advanced search window appears. Enter your search terms in the **Find** field. Your search terms can be keywords or selections from search history. Boolean operators (AND, OR, NOT) can also be included in your search.

You can also use **field codes** with your search terms. Fields refer to searchable aspects of an article or Web page; in the case of ContentSelect, they include author, title, subject, abstract, and journal name. Click **Field Codes** to display a list of field codes available with the databases you are using. Type the field code before your search terms to limit those words to the field you entered. For example, **AU Naughton** will find records that contain Naughton in the author field.

To **print, e-mail, or save** several search results, click on the folder next to the result; then print, e-mail, or save from the folder at the top of the results field. (You can still print, e-mail, or save individual results from the open article or citation.)

You can remove specific results, or clear the entire folder and collect new results, during your session. If you end your session, or it times out due to inactivity, the folder is automatically cleared.

Full-Text Results.   Some ContentSelect results will be available in full text—that is, if you click on the full text logo at the bottom of an entry, you will be able to call up the entire journal or magazine article. If you want to limit your search to results available in full text, click on the "search options" tab, and then on "full text." Then renew your search.

Abstract and Citation Results.   Many ContentSelect results are in the form of citations containing abstracts. A **citation** is a bibliographic reference to an article or document, with basic information such as ISSN (International Standard Serial Number, the standard method for identifying publications) and publisher that will help you locate it. An **abstract** is a brief description of an article, usually written by the author. An abstract will help you decide whether you want to locate the work—either in an electronic database or a print version—through your college library.

A handy tip: once you have found an article that meets your research needs, you can search fields easily from the article citation to turn up similar articles. For example, suppose a particular 2005 story from the *Christian Science Monitor* suits your paper perfectly. Go to the citation and click on the subject field to find similar articles. Or, if you want to see what else the author has written, click on the author field to produce a list of articles he or she has written.

In many cases you can search the full text of articles using electronic databases and then read the entire article online. Typically, in order to use these databases you need to have a library card number or special password provided by the library. But sometimes when you use an electronic database you will find that the text of an article won't be accessible online, so you'll have to go to the library's shelves to find the magazine or newspaper in which the article originally appeared.

The *New York Times* Search by Subject Archive

Newspapers, also known as periodicals because they are issued in periodic installments (e.g., daily, weekly, or monthly), provide contemporary information. Information in periodicals—journals, magazines, and newspapers—may be useful, or even critical, when you are ready to focus in on specific aspects of your topic, or to find more up-to-date information.

There are some significant differences between newspaper articles and journal articles, and you should consider the level of scholarship that is most appropriate for your research. Popular or controversial topics may not be well covered in journals, even though coverage in newspapers and "general interest" magazines like *Newsweek* and *Science* for that same topic may be extensive.

ResearchNavigator.com gives you access to a one-year, "search by subject" archive of articles from one of the world's leading newspapers—*The New York Times.* To learn more about *The New York Times,* visit them on the Web at **http://www.nytimes.com**.

Using the search-by-subject archive is easy. Simply select a subject and type a word, or multiple words separated by commas, into the search box and click "go." The *New York Times* search by subject archive sorts article results by relevance, with the most relevant appearing first. To view the most recently published articles first, use the "Sort by" pull-down menu located just above the search results. You can further refine your search as needed. Articles can be printed or saved for later use in your research assignment. Be sure to review the citation rules for how to cite a newspaper article in endnotes or a bibliography.

"Best of the Web" Link Library

The third database included on ResearchNavigator.com, Link Library, is a collection of Web links, organized by academic subject and key terms. To use this database, simply select an academic subject from the dropdown list, and then find the key term for the topic you are searching. Click on the key term and see a list of five to seven editorially reviewed Web sites that offer educationally relevant and reliable content. For example, if your research topic is "Allergies," you may want to select the academic subject Biology and then click on "Allergies" for links to web sites that explore this topic. Simply click on the alphabet bar to view other key terms in Biology, and their corresponding links. The web links in Link Library are monitored and updated each week, reducing your incidence of finding "dead" links.

International *Financial Times* Article Archive

ResearchNavigator.com's fourth database of content is the *Financial Times* Article Archive and Company Financials Database. Through an exclusive agreement with the *Financial Times,* a leading daily newspaper covering national and international news and business, you can search this publication's one-year archive for news stories affecting countries, companies, and people throughout the world. Simply enter your keyword(s) in the text box and click the **GO** button.

Using Your Library

After you have selected your topic and gathered source material from the three databases of content on ResearchNavigator.com, you may need to complete your research by going to your school library. ResearchNavigator.com does not try to replace the library, but rather helps you understand how to use library resources effectively and efficiently.

You may put off going to the library to complete research assignments or research papers because the library can seem overwhelming. ResearchNavigator.com provides a bridge to the library by taking you through a simple step-by-step overview of how to make the most of your library time. Written by a library scientist, the *Using Your Library* tab explains:

- Major types of libraries
- What the library has to offer
- How to choose the right library tools for a project
- The research process
- How to make the most of research time in the library

In addition, when you are ready to use the library to complete a research assignment or research paper, ResearchNavigator.com includes 31 discipline-specific "library guides" for you to use as a roadmap. Each guide includes an overview of the discipline's major subject databases, online journals, and key associations and newsgroups.

For more information and detailed walk-throughs, please visit
www.researchnavigator.com/about

Start Writing

Once you've become well acquainted with the steps in the research process and gathered source materials from ResearchNavigator.com and your school library, it's time to begin writing your assignment. Content found in this tab will help you do just that, beginning with a discussion on how to draft a research paper in an academic style. Other areas addressed include:

- Blending reference material into your writing
- Writing the introduction, body, and conclusion
- Revising, proofreading, and formatting the rough draft
- Online *Grammar Guide* that spells out some of the rules and conventions of standard written English. Included are guidelines and examples for good sentence structure; tips for proper use of articles, plurals and possessives, pronouns, adjectives and adverbs; details on subject-verb agreement and verb tense consistency; and help with the various forms of punctuation.

This is also the tab where you will find sample research papers for your reference. Use them as a guide to writing your own assignment.

Endnotes & Bibliography

The final step in a research assignment is to create endnotes and a bibliography. In an era dubbed "The Information Age," knowledge and words are taking on more significance than ever. Laws requiring writers to document or give credit to the sources of information, while evolving, must be followed.

Various organizations have developed style manuals detailing how to document sources in their particular disciplines. For writing in the humanities and social sciences, the Modern Language Association (MLA) and American Psychological Association (APA) guidelines are the most commonly used, but others, such as those in *The Chicago Manual of Style* (CMS), are also required. The purpose of this Research Navigator™ tab is to help you properly cite your research sources. It contains detailed information on MLA, APA, CMS, and CBE styles. You'll also find guidance on how to cite the material you've gathered right from ResearchNavigator.com!

This Research Navigator tab also provides students with the option to use ***AutoCite.*** Students just select their documentation style (MLA or APA), and then fill in the fields with information about their source. ***AutoCite*** will do the rest! It will automatically create the entry in the proper format. Once completed, ***AutoCite*** will also generate a "Works Cited" or "References" list that students can print or save (cut and paste).

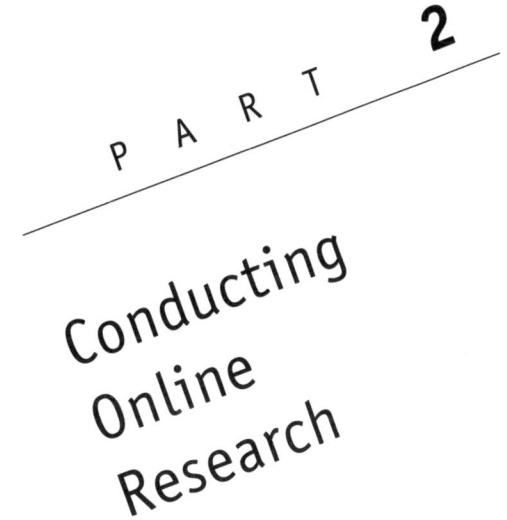

P A R T **2**

Conducting
Online
Research

Finding Sources:
Search Engines and Subject Directories

Your professor has just given you an assignment to give a five minute speech on the topic "gun control." After a (hopefully brief) panic attack, you begin to think of what type of information you need before you can write the speech. To provide an interesting introduction, you decide to involve your class by taking a straw poll of their views for and against gun control, and to follow this up by giving some statistics on how many Americans favor (and oppose) gun control legislation and then by outlining the arguments on both sides of the issue. If you already know the correct URL for an authoritative Web site like Gallup Opinion Polls (www.gallup.com) or other sites you are in great shape! However, what do you do when you don't have a clue as to which Web site would have information on your topic? In these cases, many, many people routinely (and mistakenly) go to Yahoo! and type in a single term (e.g., guns). This approach is sure to bring first a smile to your face when the results offer you 200,874 hits on your topic, but just as quickly make you grind your teeth in frustration when you start scrolling down the hit list and find sites that range from gun dealerships, to reviews of the video "Young Guns," to aging fan sites for "Guns and Roses."

Finding information on a specific topic on the Web is a challenge. The more intricate your research need, the more difficult it is to find the one or two Web sites among the billions that feature the information you want. This section is designed to help you to avoid frustration and to focus in on the right site for your research by using search engines, subject directories, and meta-sites.

Search Engines

Search engines (sometimes called search services) are becoming more numerous on the Web. Originally, they were designed to help users search the Web by topic. More recently, search engines have added features which enhance their usefulness, such as searching a particular part of the Web (e.g., only sites of educational institutions—dot.edu), retrieving just one site which the search engine touts as most relevant (like Ask.com {www.ask.com}), or retrieving up to 10 sites which the search engine rank as most relevant (like Google {www.google.com}).

Search Engine Defined

According to Cohen (1999):

> "A search engine service provides a searchable database of Internet files collected by a computer program called a wanderer, crawler, robot, worm, or spider. Indexing is created from the collected files, and the results are presented in a schematic order. There are no selection criteria for the collection of files.
>
> A search service therefore consists of three components: (1) a spider, a program that traverses the Web from link to link, identifying and reading pages; (2) an index, a database containing a copy of each Web page gathered by the spider; and (3) a search engine mechanism, software that enables users to query the index and then returns results in a schematic order (p. 31)."

One problem students often have in their use of search engines is that they are deceptively easy to use. Like our example "guns," no matter what is typed into the handy box at the top, links to numerous Web sites appear instantaneously, lulling students into a false sense of security. Since so much was retrieved, surely SOME of it must be useful. WRONG! Many Web sites retrieved will be very light on substantive content, which is not what you need for most academic endeavors. Finding just the right Web site has been likened to finding diamonds in the desert.

As you can see by the definition above, one reason for this is that most search engines use indexes developed by machines. Therefore they are indexing terms not concepts. The search engine cannot tell the difference between the keyword "crack" to mean a split in the sidewalk and "crack" referring to crack cocaine. To use search engines properly takes some skill, and this chapter will provide tips to help you use search engines more effectively. First, however, let's look at the different types of search engines with examples:

TYPES OF SEARCH ENGINES

TYPE	DESCRIPTION	EXAMPLES
1st Generation	• Non-evaluative, do not evaluate results in terms of content or authority. • Return results ranked by relevancy alone (number of times the term(s) entered appear, usually on the first paragraph or page of the site)	AltaVista (www.altavista.com) Excite (www.excite.com) HotBot (www.HotBot.com) Ixquick Metasearch (ixquick.com) Lycos (www.lycos.com)
2nd Generation	• More creative in displaying results. • Results are ordered by characteristics such as: concept, document type, Web site, popularity, etc. rather than relevancy.	Ask (www.ask.com) Direct Hit (www.directhit.com) Google! (www.google.com) HotLinks (www.hotlinks.com) Simplifind (www.simpli.com) SurfWax (www.surfwax.com) Also see Meta-Search engines below. EVALUATIVE SEARCH ENGINES About.Com (www.about.com) WebCrawler (www.webcrawler.com)
Commercial Portals	• Provide additional features such as: customized news, stock quotations, weather reports, shopping, etc. • They want to be used as a "one stop" Web guide. • They profit from prominent advertisements and fees charged to featured sites.	GONetwork (www.go.com) Google Web Directory (directory.google.com) LookSmart (www.looksmart.com) My Starting Point (www.stpt.com) Open Directory Project (dmoz.org) NetNow (www.inetnow.com) Yahoo! (www.yahoo.com)
Meta-Search Engines	Run searches on multiple search engines.	There are different types of meta-search engines. See the next 2 boxes.

(continued)

TYPES OF SEARCH ENGINES, *continued*

TYPE	DESCRIPTION	EXAMPLES
Meta-Search Engines *Integrated Result*	• Display results for search engines in one list. • Duplicates are removed. • Only portions of results from each engine are returned.	Beaucoup.com (www.beaucoup.com) Highway 61 (www.highway61.com) Cyber411 (www.cyber411. com) Mamma (www.mamma.com) MetaCrawler (www. metacrawler.com) Visisimo (www.vivisimo.com) Northern Light (www.nlsearch.com) SurfWax (www.surfwax.com)
Meta-Search Engines *Non-Integrated Results*	• Comprehensive search. • Displays results from each search engine in separate results sets. • Duplicates remain. • You must sift through all the sites.	Dogpile (www.dogpile.com) GoHip (www.gohip.com) Searchalot (www.searchalot.com) ProFusion (www. profusion.com)

QUICK TIPS FOR MORE EFFECTIVE USE OF SEARCH ENGINES

1. Use a search engine:
   - When you have a narrow idea to search.
   - When you want to search the full text of countless Web pages
   - When you want to retrieve a large number of sites
   - When the features of the search engine (like searching particular parts of the Web) help with your search

2. Always use Boolean Operators to combine terms. Searching on a single term is a sure way to retrieve a very large number of Web pages, few, if any, of which are on target.
   - Always check search engine's HELP feature to see what symbols are used for the operators as these vary (e.g., some engines use the & or + symbol for AND).
   - Boolean Operators include:
     AND to narrow search and to make sure that **both** terms are included
       e.g., children AND violence
     OR to broaden search and to make sure that **either** term is included
       e.g., child OR children OR juveniles
     NOT to **exclude** one term
       e.g., eclipse NOT lunar

3. Use appropriate symbols to indicate important terms and to indicate phrases (Best Bet for Constructing a Search According to Cohen (1999): Use a plus sign (+) in front of terms you want to retrieve: +solar +eclipse. Place a phrase in double quotation marks: "solar eclipse" Put together: "+solar eclipse" "+South America").

4. Use word stemming (a.k.a. truncation) to find all variations of a word (check search engine HELP for symbols).
   - If you want to retrieve child, child's, or children use child* (some engines use other symbols such as !, #, or $)
   - Some engines automatically search singular and plural terms, check HELP to see if yours does.

5. Since search engines only search a portion of the Web, use several search engines or a meta-search engine to extend your reach.

6. Remember search engines are generally mindless drones that do not evaluate. Do not rely on them to find the best Web sites on your topic, use *subject directories* or meta-sites to enhance value (see below).

Finding Those Diamonds in the Desert: Using Subject Directories and Meta-sites

Although some search engines, like WebCrawler (www.webcrawler. com) do evaluate the Web sites they index, most search engines do not make any judgment on the worth of the content. They just return a long—sometimes very long—list of sites that contained your keyword. However, *subject directories* exist that are developed by human indexers, usually librarians or subject experts, and are defined by Cohen (1999) as follows:

> "A subject directory is a service that offers a collection of links to Internet resources submitted by site creators or evaluators and organized into subject categories. Directory services use selection criteria for choosing links to include, though the selectivity varies among services (p. 27)."

World Wide Web Subject directories are useful when you want to see sites on your topic that have been reviewed, evaluated, and selected for their authority, accuracy, and value. They can be real time savers for students, since subject directories weed out the commercial, lightweight, or biased Web sites.

Metasites are similar to subject directories, but are more specific in nature, usually dealing with one scholarly field or discipline. Some examples of subject directories and meta-sites are found in the table on the next page.

SMART SEARCHING—SUBJECT DIRECTORIES AND META-SITES

TYPES—SUBJECT DIRECTORIES	EXAMPLES
General, covers many topics	Access to Internet and Subject Resources (www2.lib.udel.edu/subj/) Best Information on the Net (BIOTN) (http://library.sau.edu/bestinfo/) INFOMINE: Scholarly Internet Resource Collections (http://infomine.ucr.edu/) Librarian's Index to the Internet (www.lii.org/) Martindale's "The Reference Desk" (www.martindalecenter.com) PINAKES: A Subject Launchpad (www.hw.ac.uk/libWWW/irn/pinakes/pinakes.html) Refdesk.com (www.refdesk.com) Search Engines and Subject Directories (College of New Jersey) (www.tcnj.edu/~library/research/internet_search.html) Scout Report Archives (www.scout.cs.wisc.edu/archives) WWW Virtual Library (http://vlib.org)
Subject Oriented	
• Communication Studies	The Media and Communication Studies Site (www.aber.ac.uk/media) University of Iowa Department of Communication Studies (www.uiowa.edu/~commstud/resources)
• Cultural Studies	Sara Zupko's Cultural Studies Center (www.popcultures.com)
• Education	Educational Virtual Library (www.csu.edu.au/education/library.html) ERIC [Education ResourcesInformation Center] (www.eduref.org) Kathy Schrock's Guide for Educators (http://kathyschrock.net/abceval/index.htm)
• Journalism	Journalism Resources (https://bailiwick.lib.uiowa.edu/journalism/) Journalism and Media Criticism page (www.chss.montclair.edu/english/furr/media.html)
• Literature	Norton Web Source to American Literature (www.wwnorton.com/naal) Project Gutenberg [Over 3,000 full text titles] (www.gutenberg.org)

SMART SEARCHING, *continued*

TYPES—SUBJECT DIRECTORIES	EXAMPLES
• Medicine & Health	PubMed [National Library of Medicine's index to Medical journals, 1966 to present] (www.ncbi.nlm.nih.gov/PubMed/) RxList: The Internet Drug Index (http://rxlist.com) Go Ask Alice (www.goaskalice.columbia.edu) [Health and sexuality]
• Technology	CNET.com (www.cnet.com)

Choose subject directories to ensure that you are searching the highest quality Web pages. As an added bonus, subject directories periodically check Web links to make sure that there are fewer dead ends and out-dated links.

Another closely related group of sites are the *Virtual Library sites,* also referred to as Digital Library sites (see the table below). Hopefully, your campus library has an outstanding Web site for both on-campus and off-campus access to resources. If not, there are

VIRTUAL LIBRARY SITES

PUBLIC LIBRARIES

• Internet Public Library	www.ipl.org
• Library of Congress	http://lcweb.loc.gov/homepage/lchp.html
• New York Public Library	www.nypl.org

University/College Libraries
• Case Western	www.cwru.edu/uclibraries.html
• Dartmouth	www.dartmouth.edu/~library
• Duke	www.lib.duke.edu/
• Franklin & Marshall	www.library.fandm.edu
• Harvard	www.harvard.edu/museums/
• Penn State	www.libraries.psu.edu
• Stanford	www.slac.stanford.edu/FIND/spires.html
• ULCA	www.library.ucla.edu

Other
• Perseus Project [subject specific— classics, supported by grants from corporations and educational institutions]	www.perseus.tufts.edu

several virtual library sites that you can use, although you should realize that some of the resources would be subscription based, and not accessible unless you are a student of that particular university or college. These are useful because, like the subject directories and meta-sites, experts have organized Web sites by topic and selected only those of highest quality.

You now know how to search for information and use search engines more effectively. In the next section, you will learn more tips for evaluating the information that you found.

BIBLIOGRAPHY FOR FURTHER READING

Books

Basch, Reva. (1996). *Secrets of the Super Net Searchers.*

Berkman, Robert I. (2000). *Find It Fast: How to Uncover Expert Information on Any Subject Online or in Print.* NY: HarperResource.

Glossbrenner, Alfred & Glossbrenner, Emily. (1999). *Search Engines for the World Wide Web,* 2nd Ed. Berkeley, CA: Peachpit Press.

Hock, Randolph, & Berinstein, Paula. (1999). *The Extreme Searcher's Guide to Web Search Engines: A Handbook for the Serious Searcher.* Information Today, Inc.

Miller, Michael. (2000). *Complete Idiot's Guide to Yahoo!* Indianapolis, IN: Que.

Miller, Michael. (2000). *Complete Idiot's Guide to Online Search Secrets.* Indianapolis, IN: Que.

Paul, Nora, Williams, Margot, & Hane, Paula. (1999). *Great Scouts!: Cyber-Guides for Subject Searching on the Web.* Information Today, Inc.

Radford, Marie, Barnes, Susan, & Barr, Linda. (2001). *Web Research: Selecting, Evaluating, and Citing* Boston. Allyn and Bacon.

Journal Articles

Cohen, Laura B. (1999, August). The Web as a research tool: Teaching strategies for instructors. *CHOICE Supplement 3,* 20–44.

Cohen, Laura B. (August 2000). Searching the Web: The Human Element Emerges. *CHOICE Supplement 37,* 17–31.

Introna, Lucas D., & Nissenbaum, Helen. (2000). Shaping the web: Why the politics of search engines matters. The Information Society, Vol. 16, No. 3, pp. 169–185.

Evaluating Sources on the Web

Congratulations! You've found a great Web site. Now what? The Web site you found seems like the perfect Web site for your research.

But, are you sure? Why is it perfect? What criteria are you using to determine whether this Web site suits your purpose?

Think about it. Where else on earth can anyone "publish" information regardless of the *accuracy, currency,* or *reliability* of the information? The Internet has opened up a world of opportunity for posting and distributing information and ideas to virtually everyone, even those who might post misinformation for fun, or those with ulterior motives for promoting their point of view. Armed with the information provided in this guide, you can dig through the vast amount of useless information and misinformation on the World Wide Web to uncover the valuable information. Because practically anyone can post and distribute their ideas on the Web, you need to develop a new set of *critical thinking skills* that focus on the evaluation of the quality of information, rather than be influenced and manipulated by slick graphics and flashy moving java script.

Before the existence of online sources, the validity and accuracy of a source was more easily determined. For example, in order for a book to get to the publishing stage, it must go through many critiques, validation of facts, reviews, editorial changes and the like. Ownership of the information in the book is clear because the author's name is attached to it. The publisher's reputation is on the line too. If the book turns out to have incorrect information, reputations and money can be lost. In addition, books available in a university library are further reviewed by professional librarians and selected for library purchase because of their accuracy and value to students. Journal articles downloaded or printed from online subscription services, such as Infotrac, ProQuest, EbscoHost, or other fulltext databases, are put through the same scrutiny as the paper versions of the journals.

On the World Wide Web, however, Internet service providers (ISPs) simply give Web site authors a place to store information. The Web site author can post information that may not be validated or tested for accuracy. One mistake students typically make is to assume that all information on the Web is of equal value. Also, in the rush to get assignments in on time, students may not take the extra time to make sure that the information they are citing is accurate. It is easy just to cut and paste without really thinking about the content in a critical way. However, to make sure you are gathering accurate information and to get the best grade on your assignments, it is vital that you develop your critical ability to sift through the dirt to find the diamonds.

Web Evaluation Criteria

So, here you are, at this potentially great site. Let's go though some ways you can determine if this site is one you can cite with confidence in your research. Keep in mind, ease of use of a Web site is an

Evaluating Web Sites Using
Five Criteria to Judge Web Site Content

Accuracy—How reliable is the information?

Authority—Who is the author and what are his or her credentials?

Objectivity—Does the Web site present a balanced or biased point of view?

Coverage—Is the information comprehensive enough for your needs?

Currency—Is the Web site up to date?

Use additional criteria to judge Web site content, including

• **Publisher, documentation, relevance, scope, audience, appropriateness of format,** and **navigation**
• Judging whether the site is made up of **primary (original) or secondary (interpretive) sources**
• Determining whether the information is **relevant** to your research

issue, but more important is learning how to determine the validity of data, facts, and statements for your use. The five traditional ways to verify a paper source can also be applied to your Web source: *accuracy, authority, objectivity, coverage,* and *currency.*

Content Evaluation

Accuracy.   Internet searches are not the same as searches of library databases because much of the information on the Web has not been edited, whereas information in databases has. It is your responsibility to make sure that the information you use in a school project is accurate. When you examine the content on a Web site or Web page, you can ask yourself a number of questions to determine whether the information is accurate.

1. Is the information reliable?
2. Do the facts from your other research contradict the facts you find on this Web page?
3. Do any misspellings and/or grammar mistakes indicate a hastily put together Web site that has not been checked for accuracy?
4. Is the content on the page verifiable through some other source? Can you find similar facts elsewhere (journals, books, or other online sources) to support the facts you see on this Web page?
5. Do you find links to other Web sites on a similar topic? If so, check those links to ascertain whether they back up the information you see on the Web page you are interested in using.
6. Is a bibliography of additional sources for research provided? Lack of a bibliography doesn't mean the page isn't accurate, but

having one allows you further investigation points to check the information.

7. Does the site of a research document or study explain how the data was collected and the type of research method used to interpret the data?

If you've found a site with information that seems too good to be true, it may be. You need to verify information that you read on the Web by crosschecking against other sources.

Authority. An important question to ask when you are evaluating a Web site is, "Who is the author of the information?" Do you know whether the author is a recognized authority in his or her field? Biographical information, references to publications, degrees, qualifications, and organizational affiliations can help to indicate an author's authority. For example, if you are researching the topic of laser surgery citing a medical doctor would be better than citing a college student who has had laser surgery.

The organization sponsoring the site can also provide clues about whether the information is fact or opinion. Examine how the information was gathered and the research method used to prepare the study or report. Other questions to ask include:

1. Who is responsible for the content of the page? Although a webmaster's name is often listed, this person is not necessarily responsible for the content.
2. Is the author recognized in the subject area? Does this person cite any other publications he or she has authored?
3. Does the author list his or her background or credentials (e.g., Ph.D. degree, title such as professor, or other honorary or social distinction)?
4. Is there a way to contact the author? Does the author provide a phone number or email address?
5. If the page is mounted by an organization, is it a known, reputable one?
6. How long has the organization been in existence?
7. Does the URL for the Web page end in the extension .edu or .org? Such extensions indicate authority compared to dotcoms (.com), which are commercial enterprises. (For example, www.cancer.com takes you to an online drugstore that has a cancer information page; www.cancer.org is the American Cancer Society Web site.)

A good idea is to ask yourself whether the author or organization presenting the information on the Web is an authority on the subject. If the answer is no, this may not be a good source of information.

Objectivity. Every author has a point of view, and some views are more controversial than others. Journalists try to be objective by providing both sides of a story. Academics attempt to persuade readers by presenting a logical argument, which cites other scholars' work. You need to look for two sided arguments in news and information sites. For academic papers, you need to determine how the paper fits within its discipline and whether the author is using controversial methods for reporting a conclusion.

Authoritative authors situate their work within a larger discipline. This background helps readers evaluate the author's knowledge on a particular subject. You should ascertain whether the author's approach is controversial and whether he or she acknowledges this. More important, is the information being presented as fact or opinion? Authors who argue for their position provide readers with other sources that support their arguments. If no sources are cited, the material may be an opinion piece rather than an objective presentation of information. The following questions can help you determine objectivity:

1. Is the purpose of the site clearly stated, either by the author or the organization authoring the site?
2. Does the site give a balanced viewpoint or present only one side?
3. Is the information directed toward a specific group of viewers?
4. Does the site contain advertising?
5. Does the copyright belong to a person or an organization?
6. Do you see anything to indicate who is funding the site?

Everyone has a point of view. This is important to remember when you are using Web resources. A question to keep asking yourself is, What is the bias or point of *view* being expressed here?

Coverage. Coverage deals with the breadth and depth of information presented on a Web site. Stated another way, it is about how much information is presented and how detailed the information is. Looking at the site map or index can give you an idea about how much information is contained on a site. This isn't necessarily bad. Coverage is a criteria that is tied closely to *your* research requirement. For one assignment, a given Web site may be too general for your needs. For another assignment, that same site might be perfect. Some sites contain very little actual information because pages are filled with links to other sites. Coverage also relates to objectivity. You should ask the following questions about coverage:

1. Does the author present both sides of the story or is a piece of the story missing?

2. Is the information comprehensive enough for your needs?
3. Does the site cover too much, too generally?
4. Do you need more specific information than the site can provide?
5. Does the site have an objective approach?

In addition to examining what is covered on a Web site, equally revealing is what is not covered. Missing information can reveal a bias in the material. Keep in mind that you are evaluating the information on a Web site for your research requirements.

Currency.   Currency questions deal with the timeliness of information. However, currency is more important for some topics than for others. For example, currency is essential when you are looking for technology related topics and current events. In contrast, currency may not be relevant when you are doing research on Plato or Ancient Greece. In terms of Web sites, currency also pertains to whether the site is being kept up to date and links are being maintained. Sites on the Web are sometimes abandoned by their owners. When people move or change jobs, they may neglect to remove theft site from the company or university server. To test currency ask the following questions:

1. Does the site indicate when the content was created?
2. Does the site contain a last revised date? How old is the date? (In the early part of 2001, a university updated their Web site with a "last updated" date of 1901! This obviously was a Y2K problem, but it does point out the need to be observant of such things!)
3. Does the author state how often he or she revises the information? Some sites are on a monthly update cycle (e.g., a government statistics page).
4. Can you tell specifically what content was revised?
5. Is the information still useful for your topic? Even if the last update is old, the site might still be worthy of use *if* the content is still valid for your research.

Relevancy to Your Research: Primary versus Secondary Sources

Some research assignments require the use of primary (original) sources. Materials such as raw data, diaries, letters, manuscripts, and original accounts of events can be considered primary material. In most cases, these historical documents are no longer copyrighted. The Web is a great source for this type of resource.

Information that has been analyzed and previously interpreted is considered a secondary source. Sometimes secondary sources are more appropriate than primary sources. If, for example, you are asked to analyze a topic or to find an analysis of a topic, a secondary source of an analysis would be most appropriate. Ask yourself the following questions to determine whether the Web site is relevant to your research:

1. Is it a primary or secondary source?
2. Do you need a primary source?
3. Does the assignment require you to cite different types of sources? For example, are you supposed to use at least one book, one journal article, and one Web page?

You need to think critically, both visually and verbally, when evaluating Web sites. Because Web sites are designed as multimedia hypertexts, nonlinear texts, visual elements, and navigational tools are added to the evaluation process.

Help in Evaluating Web Sites.   One shortcut to finding high-quality Web sites is using subject directories and meta-sites, which select the Web sites they index by similar evaluation criteria to those just described. If you want to learn more about evaluating Web sites, many colleges and universities provide sites that help you evaluate Web resources. The following list contains some excellent examples of these evaluation sites:

• Evaluating Quality on the Net—Hope Tillman, Babson College
  www.hopetillman.com/findqual.html
• Critical Web Evaluation—Kurt W. Wagner, William Paterson University of New Jersey
  http://euphrates.wpunj.edu/faculty/wagnerk/
• Evalation Criteria—Susan Beck, New Mexico State University
  http://lib.nmsu.edu/instruction/evalcrit.html
• A Student's Guide to Research with the WWW
  www.slu.edu/departments/english/research/

Critical Evaluation Web Sites

WEB SITE AND URL	SOURCE
Critical Thinking in an Online World **www.library.ucsb.edu/untangle/jones.html**	*Paper from "Untangling the Web" 1996*
Educom Review: Information **www.educause.edu/pub/er/review/reviewArticles/31231.html**	*EDUCAUSE Literacy as a Liberal Art (1996 article)*

WEB SITE AND URL	SOURCE
Evaluating Web Sites **www.lib.purdue.edu/InternetEval**	*Purdue University Library*
Searching the Web **www.lehigh.edu/helpdesk/ useweb.html**	*Lehigh University*
Kathy Schrock's ABC's of Web Site Evaluation **www.kathyschrock.net/abceval/**	*Author's Web site*
Testing the Surf: Criteria for Evaluating Internet Information Sources **http://info.lib.uh.edu/pr/v8/n3/ smit8n3.html**	*University of Houston Libraries*
UCLA College Library Instruction: Thinking Critically about World Wide Web Resources **www.library.ucla.edu/libraries/ college/help/critical/**	*UCLA Library*
UG OOL: Judging Quality on the Internet **www.open.uoguelph.ca/resources/ skills/judging.html**	*University of Guelph*
Web Evaluation Criteria **http://lib.nmsu.edu/instruction/ evalcrit.html**	*New Mexico State University Library*
Web Page Credibility Checklist **www.park.pvt.k12.md.us/academics/ research/credcheck.htm**	*Park School of Baltimore*
Evaluating Web Sites for Educational Uses: Bibliography and Checklist **www.unc.edu/cit/guides/irg-49.html**	*University of North Carolina*
Evaluating Web Sites **www.lesley.edu/library/guides/ research/evaluating_web.html**	*Lesley University*

Tip: Can't seem to get a URL to work? If the URL doesn't begin with www, you may need to put the http:// in front of the URL. Usually, browsers can handle URLs that begin with www without the need to type in the "http://" but if you find you're having trouble, add the http://.

Documentation Guidelines for Online Sources

Your Citation for Exemplary Research

There's another detail left for us to handle—the formal citing of electronic sources in academic papers. The very factor that makes research on the Internet exciting is the same factor that makes referencing these sources challenging: their dynamic nature. A journal article exists, either in print or on microfilm, virtually forever. A document on the Internet can come, go, and change without warning. Because the purpose of citing sources is to allow another scholar to retrace your argument, a good citation allows a reader to obtain information from your primary sources, to the extent possible. This means you need to include not only information on when a source was posted on the Internet (if available) but also when you obtained the information.

The two arbiters of form for academic and scholarly writing are the Modern Language Association (MLA) and the American Psychological Association (APA); both organizations have established styles for citing electronic publications.

MLA Style

In the fifth edition of the *MLA Handbook for Writers of Research Papers,* the MLA recommends the following formats:

- **URLs:** URLs are enclosed in angle brackets (<>) and contain the access mode identifier, the formal name for such indicators as "http" or "ftp." If a URL must be split across two lines, break it only after a slash (/). Never introduce a hyphen at the end of the first line. The URL should include all the parts necessary to identify uniquely the file/document being cited.

    <http://www.csun.edu/~rtvfdept/home/index.html>

- **An online scholarly project or reference database:** A complete "online reference contains the title of the project or database (underlined); the name of the editor of the project or database (if given); electronic publication information, including version number (if relevant and if not part of the title), date of electronic publication or latest update, and name of any sponsoring institution or organization; date of access; and electronic address.

    The Perseus Project. Ed. Gregory R. Crane.
        Mar. 1997. Department of Classics,
        Tufts University. 15 June 1998 <http://
        www.perseus.tufts.edu/>.

If you cannot find some of the information, then include the information that is available. The MLA also recommends that you print or download electronic documents, freezing them in time for future reference.

- **A document within a scholarly project or reference database:** It is much more common to use only a portion of a scholarly project or database. To cite an essay, poem, or other short work, begin this citation with the name of the author and the title of the work (in quotation marks). Then, include all the information used when citing a complete online scholarly project or reference database, however, make sure you use the URL of the specific work and not the address of the general site.

Cuthberg, Lori. "Moonwalk: Earthlings' Finest Hour." <u>Discovery Channel Online</u>. 1999. Discovery Channel. 25 Nov. 1999 <http:// www.discovery.com/indep/newsfeatures/ moonwalk/challenge.html>.

- **A professional or personal site:** Include the name of the person creating the site (reversed), followed by a period, the title of the site (underlined), or, if there is no title, a description such as Home page (such a description is neither placed in quotes nor underlined). Then, specify the name of any school, organization, or other institution affiliated with the site and follow it with your date of access and the URL of the page.

Packer, Andy. Home page. 1Apr. 1998 <http:// www.suu.edu/~students/Packer.htm>.

Some electronic references are truly unique to the online domain. These include email, newsgroup postings, MUDs (multiuser domains) or MOOs (multiuser domains, object-oriented), and IRCs (Internet Relay Chats).

Email. In citing email messages, begin with the writer's name (reversed) followed by a period, then the title of the message (if any) in quotations as it appears in the subject line. Next comes a description of the message, typically "Email to," and the recipient (e.g., "the author"), and finally the date of the message.

Davis, Jeffrey. "Web Writing Resources." Email to Nora Davis. 3 Jan. 2000.

Sommers, Laurice. "Re: College Admissions Practices." Email to the author. 12 Aug. 1998.

List Servers and Newsgroups.   In citing these references, begin with the author's name (reversed) followed by a period. Next include the title of the document (in quotes) from the subject line, followed by the words "Online posting" (not in quotes). Follow this with the date of posting. For list servers, include the date of access, the name of the list (if known), and the online address of the list's moderator or administrator. For newsgroups, follow "Online posting" with the date of posting, the date of access, and the name of the newsgroup, prefixed with "news:" and enclosed in angle brackets.

Applebaum, Dale. "Educational Variables." Online
    posting. 29 Jan. 1998. Higher Education Dis-
    cussion Group. 30 Jan. 1993 <jlucidoj@unc.edu>.

Gostl, Jack. "Re: Mr. Levitan." Online posting.
    13 June 1997. 20 June 1997 <news:alt.edu.
    bronxscience>.

MUDs, MOOs, and IRCs.   Begin with the name of the speaker(s) followed by a period. Follow with the description and date of the event, the forum in which the communication took place, the date of access, and the online address. If you accessed the MOO or MUD through telnet, your citation might appear as follows:

Guest. Personal interview. 13 Aug. 1998.
    <telnet://du.edu:8888>.

For more information on MLA documentation style for online sources, check out their Web site at http://www.mla.org/style/sources.htm.

APA Style

The newly revised *Publication Manual of the American Psychological Association* (5th ed.) now includes guidelines for Internet resources. The manual recommends that, at a minimum, a reference of an Internet source should provide a document title or description, a date (either the date of publication or update or the date of retrieval), and an address (in Internet terms, a uniform resource locator, or URL). Whenever possible, identify the authors of a document as well. It's important to remember that, unlike the MLA, the APA does not include temporary or transient sources (e.g., letters, phone calls, etc.) in its "References" page, preferring to handle them in the text. The general suggested format is as follows:

Online periodical:

Author, A. A., Author, B. B., & Author,
    C. C. (2000). Title of article. *Title of*
    Periodical, xx, xxxxx. Retrieved month, day,
    year, from source.

Online document:

Author, A. A. (2000). *Title of work*. Retrieved
    month, day, year, from source.

Some more specific examples are as follows:

FTP (File Transfer Protocol) Sites. To cite files available for downloading via FTP, give the author's name (if known), the publication date (if available and if different from the date accessed), the full title of the paper (capitalizing only the first word and proper nouns), the date of access, and the address of the FTP site along with the full path necessary to access the file.

Deutsch, P. (1991) Archie: An electronic
    directory service for the Internet. Retrieved
    January 25, 2000 from File Transfer Protocol:
    ftp://ftp.sura.net/pub/archie/docs/
    whatis.archie

WWW Sites (World Wide Web). To cite files available for viewing or downloading via the World Wide Web, give the author's name (if known), the year of publication (if known and if different from the date accessed), the full title of the article, and the title of the complete work (if applicable) in italics. Include any additional information (such as versions, editions, or revisions) in parentheses immediately following the title. Include the date of retrieval and full URL (the http address).

Burka, L. P. (1993). A hypertext history of
    multi-user dungeons. *MUDdex*. Retrieved
    January 13, 1997 from the World Wide Web:
    http://www.utopia.com/talent/lpb/muddex/essay/

Tilton, J. (1995). Composing good HTML (Vers.
    2.0.6). Retrieved December 1, 1996 from the
    World Wide Web: http://www.cs.cmu.edu/
    ~tilt/cgh/

Synchronous Communications (MOOs, MUDs, IRC, etc.). Give
the name of the speaker(s), the complete date of the conversation
being referenced in parentheses, and the title of the session (if applicable). Next, list the title of the site in italics, the protocol and
address (if applicable), and any directions necessary to access the
work. Last, list the date of access, followed by the retrieval information. Personal interviews do not need to be listed in the References,
but do need to be included in parenthetic references in the text (see
the APA *Publication Manual*).

Cross, J. (1996, February 27). Netoric's Tuesday
    "cafe: Why use MUDs in the writing classroom?
    MediaMoo. Retrieved March 1, 1996 from File
    Transfer Protocol: ftp://daedalus.com/pub/
    ACW/NETORIC/catalog

Gopher Sites.   List the author's name (if applicable), the year
of publication, the title of the file or paper, and the title of the
complete work (if applicable). Include any print publication information (if available) followed by the protocol (i.e., gopher://). List
the date that the file was accessed and the path necessary to access
the file.

Massachusetts Higher Education Coordinating
    Council. (1994). Using coordination and
    collaboration to address change. Retrieved
    July 16, 1999 from the World Wide Web:
    gopher://gopher.mass.edu:170/
    00gopher_root%3A%5B_hecc%5D_plan

Email, Listservs, and Newsgroups.   Do not include personal
email in the list of References. Although unretrievable communication such as email is not included in APA References, somewhat more
public or accessible Internet postings from newsgroups or listservs
may be included. See the APA *Publication Manual* for information
on in-text citations.

Heilke, J. (1996, May 3). Webfolios. Alliance
    for Computers and Writing Discussion List.
    Retrieved December 31, 1996 from the World
    Wide Web: http://www.ttu.edu/lists/acw-l/
    9605/0040.html

Other authors and educators have proposed similar extensions to the APA style. You can find links to these pages at:

www.psychwww.com/resource/apacrib.htm

Remember, "frequently-referenced" does not equate to "correct" "or even "desirable." Check with your professor to see if your course or school has a preference for an extended APA style.

PART 3

Research Tips for Speech Communication

In Part I, you were introduced to ResearchNavigator.com and to ways to use it to conduct research on any topic or academic discipline. In Part II, we reviewed many types of search engines and how to evaluate and cite sources found on line. In this Part, we will focus specifically on the discipline of communication.

We will concentrate on using the resources within Research Navigator.com to conduct a number of typical searches that are often required to fulfill assignments in speech communication courses. These assignments may require you to write a research paper, deliver a speech, or to participate in a symposium. Regardless of the course or the assignment, the one thing that many assignments in college have in common is that they require you to do research.

A major advantage of using ResearchNavigator.com to conduct your research is that all of the information that it leads to has been reviewed by editors of the various peer reviewed journals, The *New York Times* or the *Financial Times*. This will give you a degree of confidence in the veracity of what you assert and the conclusions you reach.

Every academic discipline covers a wide body of information. Most of the people using this version of the ResearchNavigator.com Guide are probably taking one of several courses. If you are taking an introductory communication course, it may be called Introduction to Human Communication, Interpersonal Communication, Group Communication, or Public Speaking. What follows are several searches on topics that may arise in the course you are currently taking.

Sample Searches

As we conduct these searches, we will focus on issues central to the field of speech communication. The results of these searches will provide information that should be of value to you as you progress through your course this semester. The goal is to teach you tools and techniques so you are able to use ResearchNavigator.com to conduct research on any topic. You are not restricted to only using the tool to conduct research for your communication course. As we work through these examples, you should think of the other assignments that you have this term that would benefit from the quality research sources that are contained within.

Communication Differs Between Genders.   We all know that men and women are different in many ways. In general, men are taller than women; women perform better in school. So, do men and women communicate in different ways, and if so, how and why? Your textbook may suggest many related areas of inquiry that you would like to consider further. This inquiry might be undertaken just for the sake of learning, or it might be the point of departure for a successful paper, report, or speech in your communication class this term.

The Link Library

If you want to use this topic as a springboard for a paper, report, or a speech you can start with the "Best of the Web" Link Library. Use the drop down menu to search the discipline of Anthropology. (NOTE: Many of the communication issues are housed in other disciplines. You should explore broadly. In addition to anthropology, you will find the subjects of business law, marketing, political science, psychology, and sociology particularly useful in finding information on communication. Of course, the discipline of English-English Composition will assist you as you prepare written work.

After clicking to the page for anthropology, use the alphabet label "G" to get to the page for "gender issues." The page will contain the following:

PUBLIC SITES:

Gender Issues Home Page

Resource for exploring issues focusing on gender and society, gender studies, gender in medicine, and more. Links to bibliographic and electronic reference materials. Site maintained by South Dakota School of Mines and Technology.

Definition of Gender Studies

Marietta College's explanation of the field and of its course offerings in this area, with links to additional course descriptions. Site maintained by Marietta College.

United Nations Gender in Development Programme

Home page for the United Nations program involved in gender and development issues. Site maintained by The United Nations.

Gender and Moral Theory

PowerPoint presentation by Lawrence Hinman at the University of San Diego explores the Kohlberg-Gilligan debate pertaining to moral reasoning and gender.

Gender in Picture Books

An analysis of gender in children's picture books. Site managed by Rutgers University.

Gender Issues in Children's Literature

The ERIC Digest is the source for this site devoted to gender portrayal in children's literature. Site hosted by Indiana University.

Maintaining Self-Esteem

This three-part essay explores different ways to help girls maintain their self-esteem when they reach adolescence, a time when girls often experience a decline in self-esteem. Site managed by Seconds, a nonprofit organization.

Empowering Girls

Professor Kay E. Vandergrift from Rutgers University explores different ways to empower girls through literature and other classroom activities.

Women's Literature

The Victorian Web addresses Elaine Showalter's A Literature of Their Own, which looks at three stages in the history of women's literature as it relates to feminist theory. Site maintained by the National University of Singapore.

Cultural Differences in Communication

Essay examines differences in gender communication. Site managed by the Electronic Frontier Foundation.

Gender Differences and Instructional Discrimination in the Classroom

Carolyn Butcher Dickman (Radford University) authored this paper entitled 'Gender Differences and Instructional Discrimination in the Classroom.' This paper is hosted online by the International Alliance for Invitational Education.

Gender-Role Development

Overview of various theories that explain the development of gender behaviors and roles. Site managed by the University of North Carolina, Chapel Hill.

Girls and Violence

Current statistics indicate that girls are quickly closing the gender gap when it comes to issues of violence and crime. This study of girls, violence, and crime is hosted by the American Bar Association.

Gender Issues

From the University of Maryland's Women's Studies database, a variety of essays covering topics associated with gender issues.

You see that there are links to over a dozen web sites that have been reviewed by the authors and Pearson Education. Unlike a standard "web search" with *Google* or *Yahoo!*, these sites have been selected for academic relevance and are brought to you without advertising. They also tend to be more focused on the type of information that you would need for your courses in college.

General Search Engines

You should compare the use of the Link Library with just doing a standard web search with a tool such as *Google* or *Yahoo!*. Try a search with your favorite search engine using the search argument "gender differences in communication" As of the writing of this book, Summer 2006, you would have found the following number of hits:

Google.com	23,300,000
Yahoo.com	2,410,000
Ask.com	724,700
About.com	143
Metacrawler.com	90
Dogpile.com	88

Sometimes, less is more! Clearly, you will not browse the millions of web sites that *Google* or *Yahoo!* find. One way to be more precise in your search strategy is to use synonyms for some of the terms. You can also expand or contact the search with the aid of tools on the search site. Ask.com, Dogpile.com, and Metacrawler.com all provide tools that offer guidance as you refine your search.

Among the sites noted in the Link Library is one titled "Cultural Differences in Communication." Before you click on the link, you can read something about it. In this case, you will see that it refers to an essay that "examines differences in gender communication." Sounds promising. Clicking on the link will take you directly to the essay by Professor Becky Michele Mulvaney of the Communication Department at Florida Atlantic University. As you read the article, you find that the author treats the differences between the genders in terms of the intercultural differences. She claims the way we are brought up as men or women, within our unique cultures, largely accounts for the differences that are noted in the way the genders communicate. It is not something hard-wired into our bodies or minds that we are born with. Thinking about the differences between the sexes as being learned (cultural) rather than predetermined (biology) is certainly an important distinction that goes beyond just observing that men and women communicate differently.

Current News Sources

After reading this article, and perhaps a few more, you may want to see if the topic of "gender communication" has been in the news recently. You can easily do this search at the *New York Times*. You can use the search argument, "gender communication." If that does not provide any hits for you, you can try the two words separately or you can try synonyms, instead of communication, try language or interaction, instead of gender, try sex, male, or female. As with any bibliographic search, the key to finding the specks of gold hidden in the mountains of information is the use synonyms intelligently.

At the time of writing this guide, no articles met the criteria for a search of "gender communication." However, for the single term "gender," there were 36 articles provided. These articles include news articles, opinion/editorial pieces, and letters to the editor. Refining the search to "gender and advertising" produced a single story dealing with the different ways the genders are portrayed in advertisements. (*Men Are Becoming the Ad Target of the Gender Sneer,* By COURTNEY KANE, Published Friday, January 28, 2005.)

Another resource that you have available in the Research Navigator is the *Financial Times*. This resource is in an international newspaper dealing with business and financial issues. Initially you may not think this will be a useful source for courses in communication. If you are taking a course in interpersonal communication, you might be right. However, if you do a search on the term "communication," you will probably find the results include many articles on the telecommunication industry. In addition, if you do a search on the term "speech" or "speeches," you will probably see almost 100 articles returned. These will include many reports on speeches made by political and business leaders. You may also see articles on freedom of speech in America or other countries.

Important Journals for Speech Communication

In addition to the web links contained in the Link Library and access to article from both the *New York Times* and the *Financial Times,* the ResearchNavigator.com provides access to current magazine and scholarly journal articles via the power of EBSCO ContentSelect. Moreover, the ContentSelect service provides a powerful visual search tool that can help you both select a research topic and do the research in a way that many people find very efficient and effective. Before we describe the searching procedure with ContentSelect, we will take a moment to describe which journals can be searched.

Many of the leading journals in the field of communication are made available within ContentSelect. When you begin a search, you select one or more databases and the search term. The search is quicker this way because you will not be searching through all the available journals, only the most relevant journals. In addition to the academic journals, many leading popular magazines are also indexed by this service. A single search will return both academic and professional magazines that relate to the field of communication.

The following periodicals contain communication topics, and can be found within the communications database:

Advances in Consumer Research
Advancing the Consumer Interest
Advertising Age International
Advertising Age's Business Marketing
Advertising Age's Creativity
Aftermarket Business
American Demographics
American Film

Argumentation & Advocacy
Army Communicator
Art, Design & Communication in Higher Education
Asian Theatre Journal
Australian Screen Education
Bank Advertising News
Biography: An Interdisciplinary Quarterly

Black Issues in Higher Education
Bulletin of the Association for Business Communication
Business Communication Quarterly
Cable World
CableFAX's CableWORLD
Career World
Changing English: Studies in Culture & Education

Changing English:
  Studies in Reading &
  Culture
Cinema Journal
Communication
  Booknotes Quarterly
Communication Law &
  Policy
Communication
  Research
Communication Review
Communications News
Consumption, Markets
  & Culture
Contemporary
  Argumentation &
  Debate
Contemporary Politics
Contemporary Theatre
  Review
Continuum: Journal of
  Media & Cultural
  Studies
Critical Studies in Media
  Communication
Cultural Studies
Current Issues &
  Research in
  Advertising
Current Science
Decisions Marketing
Design Week
Dissent
Distance Learning
Drug Design &
  Discovery
E Magazine: The
  Environmental
  Magazine
Education, Communica-
  tion & Information
e-learning
Electronic Markets
FDA Consumer
Future Survey

Futures Research
  Quarterly
Global Society: Journal
  of Interdisciplinary
  International
  Relations
Health Communication
Howard Journal of
  Communications
Information &
  Communications
  Technology Law
Information
  Communication &
  Society
Information
  Infrastructure &
  Policy
Information Polity: The
  International Journal
  of Government &
  Democracy in the
  Information Age
Information Services &
  Use
Information Society
In-Store Marketing
International Journal of
  Evidence & Proof
Journal of Behavioral
  Finance
Journal of Business
  & Technical
  Communication
Journal of Business
  Communication
Journal of
  Communication
Journal of Consumer
  Psychology
Journal of Current
  Issues & Research in
  Advertising
Journal of Educational
  Media

Journal of Family
  Communication
Journal of Film & Video
Journal of Health
  Communication
Journal of Intercultural
  Communication
  Research
Journal of International
  Marketing
Journal of Language,
  Identity & Education
Journal of Marketing
  Communications
Journal of Marketing
  Research (JMR)
Journal of Mass Media
  Ethics
Journal of Media
  Economics
Journal of Media Practice
Journal of Popular Film
  & Television
Journal of Psychology
  & Financial Markets
Journal of Public
  Administration
  Research & Theory
  (Oxford University
  Press)
Journal of Public
  Administration
  Research & Theory
  (Transaction)
Journal of Public Policy
  & Marketing
Journal of Public
  Relations Research
Journal of Radio Studies
Journalism &
  Communication
  Monographs
Journalism & Mass
  Communication
  Educator

Journalism & Mass Communication Quarterly
Journalism Educator
Journalism Studies
Literature in Performance
Management Communication Quarterly
Marketing (UK)
Marketing Research
Marketing Week (UK)
Mass Communication & Society
Media History
Media Psychology
Medical Marketing & Media
Monthly Labor Review
Mother Earth News
National Interest
Network World
New Cinemas: Journal of Contemporary Film
New Media Age
New Statesman
New Yorker
News Media & the Law
Newsweek
Political Communication
Political Science Quarterly
Popular Communication

Popular Music & Society
Progressive
Public Relations Quarterly
Public Relations Research Annual
Publishing Research Quarterly
Quarterly Review of Film & Video
Radio Journal: International Studies in Broadcast & Audio Media
Reading Psychology
Research in Drama Education
Retail Merchandiser
Rhetoric Review
Satellite Broadband: The Cutting Edge of Satellite Communications
Science Communication
Scientific Studies of Reading
Screen Education
Shakespeare Studies
St. Louis Journalism Review
Stage Directions
Studies in Theatre & Performance

Technical Communication Quarterly
Technology & Health Care
Telecommunications— Americas Edition
Telecommunications— International Edition
Telephony
Trends in Communication
U.S. Department of State Dispatch
U.S. News & World Report—Blue Chip Edition
U.S. News & World Report—Executive Edition
UN Chronicle
Vanity Fair
Video Systems
Visual Resources
Visual Studies
Wireless Asia
Wireless Review
Wireless Systems Design
Women's Studies
World Health
Worldwide Biotech
Written Communication

You will see that these 153 periodicals represent a wide range of magazines and journals that always or often deal with communication issues. This database will be a wonderful place to start your research of projects this semester. However, there are several other journals that also contain communication issues, but are included in other areas, such as, psychology, sociology, or political science. We will discuss how to access the many additional journals when we describe searching the ContentSelect databases.

ContentSelect

To begin a search in ContentSelect, first select your database(s) from the drop down menu and type your search term. Let's continue with the topic of "gender and communication." Selecting the discipline of communication and the search term of "gender communication" we found 220 articles returned. The number of articles that are returned is noted at the bottom of the results page.

While this seems like it may be too many to review, before you look to narrow the search, look at the sort options. You will see that the results are originally sorted in date order with the most recent first. You may find it more useful to sort by relevance. As you review the list of articles, you will see a list of suggestions (on the left) for narrowing your search by adding additional search terms. If you add the term "sex differences," you will see the number of articles reduced considerably.

Whether you choose to review the larger list or a narrower list, you can do several things with the articles of interest. For beginners, you can see the full citation and, if available, download the entire article for viewing or saving. Moreover, you can save this information in your personal "EBSCO HOST folder." You do this by clicking on the icon on the right labeled "add." If you save it in your folder, the information will only be "saved" for the duration of the current session. To save your finds for another day, you need to sign in. The sign in procedures in noted in the upper left.

As you find articles, you will see that you have the option of see the citation and in many cases to download the entire article. Once reviewed, the citation and the article can be saved on your local computer and /or printed.

Expanding and narrowing your search

Now look at the tabs at the top of the result page. You will see there are four of them. You are already in "Basic Search." By clicking on the "Advanced Search," you will see that you can limit your search to only those articles that have the full text available online or expand the search by checking any of three ways to expand the search:

- Search for related words
- Search within the full text of articles
- Automatically use "and" between search words

In the case of the search for "gender communication", you will see that limiting the search to only full text articles reduces the number by about half. Now try expanding the search to include "search within the full text of the articles." You will probably find far larger number of hits.

In the event that you are not finding many relevant articles, you can choose another disciple database by selecting it from the drop down window. Alternatively, you can select several databases simultaneously. Just click the tab labeled "Choose Databases" and you will be able to select multiple databases. Try the search for "gender communication" using both the communication and the psychology databases. You should see that the number of hits has gone up.

Visual Searches

One additional way you can search with the ResearchNavigator.com is to do a Visual Search with EBSCO Host. Returning to our initial interest in gender communication, we may want to brainstorm as to what are the related topics for this area of inquiry. Click the tab labeled "Visual Search" and you will get another search window. Type "gender communication" in the find field you will see the results in a circular diagram on the left side of the screen. The results are a visual map that contains:

- **Circles,** which represent categories of results. Categories can include subcategory circles. Click on a circle (category) to explore its contents.
- **Squares,** which represent links to articles. Click on a square to load the article into this pane.

At the top left of the results window you will see a "Show Filters" option. With the filters, you can limit or focus information by keyword, date, or publication name. Help is available at the top right and a "tour" of the Visual Search facility is also available. You will see that the big advantage of viewing the results visually is that it is organized in a very useful manner.

Major Topics for Speech Communication

As you approach your communication course this semester, you will undoubtedly be learning new terms. Make sure that you review the chapter "key terms" or glossary in the back of the text to make sure you are familiar with the terms of the discipline. Based on the course you are taking, this set of vocabulary words may deal with the broad area of human communication or some sub areas of the communication discipline as group communication, intercultural communication, interpersonal communication, or public speaking. The course may also deal with aspects of mass media or computer mediated communication. What follows are some of the key terms from the broad area covered by many courses in speech communication. You may find these topics and the related search terms are useful as you plan your study and research this semester.

Use the search terms, along with others you may think of, to limit or expand your searches. Also, use any combination for these terms within the Visual Search tool of EBSCO Host to get additional ideas for the way the field of communication is organized.

MAJOR TOPICS	USEFUL SEARCH TERMS
Audience Analysis	Demographics
	Psychographics
	Survey
	Opinion
	Attitude
	Belief
	Behavior
Communication models	Source
	Encoding
	Message
	Decoding
	Receiver
	Channel
	Interference
	Context
Conformity	Groups
	Groups norms
	Customs
	Cultures
Credibility	Source credibility
	Competence
	Character
	Common ground
Delivery	Verbal communication
	Non-verbal communication
	Extemporaneous speaking
	Eye contact
	Gestures

Language	Semantics
	Syntax
	Pragmatics
	Natural
	Computer
Listening	Active listening
	Hearing
	Understanding
	Remembering
	Interpreting
	Evaluating
Nonverbal communication	Facial expression
	Body movement
	Touch
	Eye contact
	Territory
Perception	Selection
	Organization
	interpretation
	Self-perception
Self concept	Race
	Class
	Gender
Self-disclosure	Intimacy
	Reciprocity
	Vulnerability
Speech apprehension	Anxiety
	Positive nervousness
	Adrenalin
Verbal communication	Class
	Race
	Gender
	Culture
	Confirming messages
	Disconfirming messages
	Logic
	Reasoning

This has been a brief overview of the process of using the Research Navigator in the discipline of speech communication. We have also suggested some topics and search terms that you might wish to explore this semester as you read your textbook and get interested in some of the topics covered. In the next section, we will discuss other online resources that will prove useful as you study communication and as you seek to become a more competent communicator.

PART 4

Online Resources

Internet Sites Useful in Speech Communication

For many of the searches you do for you communication class this semester, and for many of the searches you do for other classes and at other times, you will want to go beyond the tools contained within ResearchNavigator.com. This section will assist you when you need to search far and wide on the web. The web is a big place. By last count, there were over 85 million websites worldwide. Surely, you need some guidance to search and filter all of it.

Of course, you already have a favorite search engine and search strategy. It may work for you in many cases. The items presented here are designed to provide added tools and techniques for you to learn about. Using many of these tools and approaches will make the research process easier and more productive much of the time. Take the time this term to explore these pages and search the sites described. The annotation can only hint about all that is available for your use.

To provide some focus to the review of the websites, we will focus on how to use the Internet as a public speaker. We will provide guidance to you as you concentrate on the task of speech planning, practice, and preparation. Specially, we will look at how you can use the resources of the Internet to accomplish four searching strategies:

1. Search the Web to find a speech topic.
2. Search the Web to gather supporting evidence.
3. Search the Web to use reference sources.
4. Search the Web to analyze your audience.

If you are not planning on delivering speeches this semester, do no worry. The information in this section can also apply to any paper you will have to write in any course at any time.

The listing of online resources is organized into the following categories:

- General Search Engines
- Meta Search Engines
- Topical Browsers
- Other Searching Tools
  - Internet Directories
  - Advocacy Groups
  - Books, Libraries & Reference Sources
  - Newspapers & Magazines

General Search Engines

AltaVista

www.altavista.com

This site allows you to select web site, images, audio, video or news related to your search. Also provides "Babel Fish" to translate from "any" language to "any" language. The interface is very clean and uncluttered. However, it does not list the number of hits.

Google

www.Google.com

This has become the most widely used search engine. You probably use it already, but have you looked at the "moor" link to the many other resources? Check out the wealth of specialized search tools they make available on the next page. Search for Blogs, directories, scholarly articles and more.

Lycos

www.Lycos.com

A standard website with lots of ads and "featured content" that allows searching.

Meta Search Engines

Searching the Web is just like any kind of research—the more sources you have, the better information you'll receive. Meta Search Engines gather results from the top engines in the business, and compile them to give you the best possible results for your search. It is a pretty simple equation, and it means you get all the top results from the leading search engines on the Web. Depending on your search, there are certain kinds of engines that may give you better results. To help explain this idea, here's a breakdown of some of the different kinds of search approaches that are included with some meta search websites.

Search Engines: Databases dedicated to gathering Internet Web pages, storing the results and then returning a list of pages that match a user's search. Search Engines might include *Google, Yahoo* and *Ask.com.*

Web Directories: These are sub-categorized overviews of Web sites. Generally, directories have less content than Search Engines, but they often contain very relevant sites since they are selected and categorized by editors. Web Directories often include: *About, LookSmart* and *Open Directory.*

Pay-For-Placement: These results are returned based on sponsors who pay for their placement within a relevant result set. For instance, a car parts dealer might pay to have their company's results returned when a user searched on a term related to car repair. These listings are denoted with the text "Sponsored By" to the right of the site URL. Pay-For-Placement engines include: *Overture, Sprinks* and *FindWhat.*

Vertical Search Engines (VSEs): These are engines or databases specifically designed to search for certain kinds of Web content. These categories can include photos and news content. VSEs include: *Yahoo, Ditto, NewsCrawler* and *ABCNews.*

So why would you use a meta search engine? They are often better because they have the top results from all the leading search engines rolled into one. You get the benefit of all the various types of search engines and their respective strengths compiled and returned to you quickly and easily. Simply put, they give you one place to go on the Web when you need answers. Unlike search engines, Meta Search Engines do not crawl the web themselves to build listings. Instead, they allow searches to be sent to several search engines all at once. The results are then blended together onto one page. Many have handy tools that can help refine a search.

Meta Search Engines

Dogpile

`www.dogpile.com`

Dogpile is a meta search engine that allows you to search multiple search engines at the same time. This service is operated by *Info-Space,* which also operates a family of Internet properties that includes *WebCrawler.com,* and *MetaCrawler.com* as well as the online directory sites *InfoSpace.com* and *Switchboard.com.*

Excite

`www.excite.com`

This site allows you to select web pages, images, audio, video or news related to your search. It also provides a list of related search arguments that might assist you with your research. The interface is very clean and uncluttered once you get past the first screen.

Hotbot

`www.hotbot.com`

Searches one at a time either *MSN, Ask.com,* or *Google.* This site also allows you to filter the searches by a number of parameters, such as date.

Kartoo

`http://www.kartoo.com`

If you like the idea of seeing your web results visually, this meta search site shows the results with sites being interconnected by keywords.

Lycos Retriever

`www.lycos.com/retriever.html`

This new service claims to be "Web's first information fusion engine, scouring the Web for the best information on thousands of topics and pulling it together into up-to-date, easy-to-read reports." Using advanced Natural Language Processing technology, Lycos Retriever's analysis can tell the difference between a page that just mentions a word, and a page that is dedicated to the word.

Mamma

http://www.mamma.com

Mamma.com is the mother of all meta search engines on the web. Mamma searches against a variety of major crawlers, directories and specialty search sites. This site will provide good suggestions to refine your search.

Proteus

www.thrall.org/proteus.html

Maintained by a public library, *Proteus* lets you easily send your search to one of several search engines. It also has links to search engine help pages.

SurfWax

http://www.surfwax.com

Searches against major engines or provides those who open free accounts the ability to choose from a list of hundreds. Using the "Facilitator" feature, you can preview any page in the results and see where your terms appear in the document. Using the "focus" feature, you can see sites that are similar, broader, or narrower than the results obtained.

Vivisimo

http://vivisimo.com/

Enter a search term, and *Vivisimo* will not only return matching responses from major search engines but also automatically organize the pages into categories.

Topical Browsers

About.com

www.about.com

This site use "experts" to provide information by categories. Do a search here and an "expert" will provide information and organize the results for you.

The Internet Public Library

www.ipl.org

This is s reference site maintained by students & faculty at over a dozen major universities.

Yahoo

www.yahoo.com

Yahoo! is not a search engine per se, but a directory . . . a distinction that says it all! *Yahoo!* is definitely head and shoulders above its competitors in terms of the relevance of its results, simply because EVERY site listed in *Yahoo!* has been filtered by humans to eliminate the flotsam and jetsam. A brilliant resource.

The World Wide Web Virtual Library

www.vlib.org

The WWW Virtual Library (VL) is the oldest catalogue of the Web, started by Tim Berners-Lee, the creator of HTML and of the Web itself, in 1991 at CERN in Geneva. Unlike commercial catalogues, it is run by a loose confederation of volunteers, who compile pages of key links for particular areas in which they are expert; even though it isn't the biggest index of the Web, the VL pages are widely recognised as being amongst the highest-quality guides to particular sections of the Web.

Who-Where Yellow Pages

http://www.whowhere.com

This special service within Lycos allows you to search for people, businesses, images and audio. Look up your own name and see if you are listed. Look up a business in your city, such as "pizza," to see how the yellow pages works.

Advocacy Groups

Advocacy groups are excellent sources of information.

Activism.net

http://activism.net

This site links to sites that advocate social & political action. They sites provide a great deal of one-sided information in support of their positions. This site is great for public speaking, especially persuasive speeches.

University of Michigan List of Think Tanks

http://www.lib.umich.edu/govdocs/psthink.html

This site lists individual think tanks as well as listings of think tanks. This site is good for well thought out position papers for reputable sources.

Lycos Activists

http://dir.lycos.com/Society/Activism/

Search Lycos' list of organizations, which spans a wide range of political and social concerns.

Think Tanks and Policy Institutes

http://dir.lycos.com/Society/Issues/
Policy_Institutes/

Browse an alphabetic list of policy study organizations that was developed by Lycos.

The ACLU

www.aclu.org

On most contemporary hot button legal issues, the American Civil Liberties Union has taken a stand that might start you out with choosing a legal topic. The page also provides briefs submitted by the ACLU in high profile court cases. See their "Activist Tool Kit" at their "Action Center."

The Brookings Institution

www.brookings.org

This is a very good source for topics if you are interested in domestic policy, especially economic issues. Be sure to click on its areas for policy briefs.

The Cato Institute

www.cato.org

This conservative think tank has published studies on a variety of domestic and international policy areas. The Cato Institute also offers an option to do a keyword search for topic areas.

Care2.com

`www.care2.com`

Care2.com is the largest online community for people who want to make a difference in such areas as health, human rights, and protecting the environment. Here, you can find links to action groups and petition drives.

Economic Policy Institute

`http://epinet.org/`

This non-partisan think-tank analyzes economic issues.

Speakout.com

`www.speakout.com`

Site is devoted to presenting both sides of controversial issues thus providing users with a way to become informed. Also provides several ways of users to express their opinion on the issues via petitions and debates.

Rand Corporation

`http://www.rand.org/`

Highlight its "Research Areas," and "Reports & Bookstore," for policy studies, especially on issues of national defense and international affairs.

Townhall.com

`http://www.townhall.com/`

Enter the Townhall where you can find a number of organizations that develop a conservative point of view.

Books, Libraries, and Reference Sources

Bibliomania

`http://www.bibliomania.com/`

This site provides online versions of classic works of fiction and non-fiction. There is also a section for poetry and reference works. Some of the titles are in PDF format and require the Adobe Acrobat Reader.

Books Online

http://digital.library.upenn.edu/books/

Scroll down the alphabetic list of authors. Good for finding classics that have been digitized.

Library of Congress

www.loc.gov

Go to the National Library. You can find information about exhibits at the Library as well as listing of its holdings. Click on "Library Catalog" for lists of holdings. Click on "Thomas" for information on current and pending legislation.

Libweb

http://sunsite.berkeley.edu

From Berkeley, this server provides links to hundreds of library collections around the world.

The Librarians' Index to the Internet

http://lii.org/

Enter a keyword or narrow your search to one of more than thirty categories to find the reference information you need.

Find Newspaper or Magazine Stories

The Drudge Report

http://www.drudgereport.com/

Updated daily by Matt Drudge, this list links you to headline stories and a wide variety of newspaper and wire service sources. A special feature is the set of links to syndicated columnists.

Editor and Publisher

www.editorandpublisher.com

In addition to a search feature, E & P provides tabs to a variety of resources from business to media to online. Take a tour.

Megatopia

www.magatopia.com

This site provides and extensive list and links to online versions of popular magazines that are organizes by categories. Just beware of the pop-ups.

NewsDirectory

www.newsdirectory.com

This guide to all English-language media is published worldwide. This free directory of newspapers, magazines, television stations, colleges, visitor bureaus, governmental agencies and more can help you get to where you want to go, or find sites you didn't know about. This site is logically organized so that our links can provide you with easy access to thousands of periodicals worldwide, including, 3,600 newspapers, 4,800 magazines, hundreds of television stations, plus many colleges, visitor bureaus, governmental agencies, travel links, and comics.

Pathfinder

http://www.pathfinder.com/

The Pathfinder page will help you find online editions of the various magazines that are part of the Time-Warner Network.

The Web As Participatory Democracy

As the World Wide Web has grown more popular a large number of people are making personal contributions by setting up blogs (web logs), participating in email discussion groups or listservs or participating in the creation and use of "wikis." You may have already used the most popular Wiki, which is "Wikipedia." Wikipedia are websites that are often both publicly available and editable by any user. (**www.wikipedia.org**) Here, you can search in many languages and you may enter search terms on the left or follow the categories on the top right. Following any of the links will allow you to narrow your inquiry. In addition to the many internal links to related subjects, Wikipedia also has a number of external links that broaden the information database available. If you are an expert in any subject, you can edit the pages of Wikipedia. To do so, follow the tabs at the top of the page or click on the "edit" button that appears in many places on the right side of the page.

Communicate with Others

Deja.com Archives on Google

http://groups.google.com/

This is one of the more user-friendly ways to take part in newsgroups.

Internet FAQ Archives

http://www.faqs.org/

A FAQ is a list of frequently asked questions about a newsgroup and how to participate in it. It is often useful to find the FAQ before subscribing.

Communication Institute for Online Scholarship

http://www.cios.org/

This organization sponsors "hotlines," email discussion groups that share information about communication scholarship. You can also join one of their forums. An individual or institutional membership is required for access.

RealGuide

http://guide.real.com

Daily guide to RealAudio and RealVideo programming in news, entertainment and sports. In addition, there is a calendar of events for the entire upcoming month.

Government Sources

AOL Government Guide

www.statelocalgov.net/index.cfm

This site provides user friendly access to government resources and services.

FEDSTATS

www.fedstats.gov/

This site is maintained by the Federal Interagency Council on Statistical Policy. You can find statistics from over 70 federal agencies.

FedWorld Information Network

www.fedworld.gov/

Developed by NTIS (National Technology Information System) this is an excellent source for finding a host of government sources.

National Archives and Records Administration

www.nara.gov/

"NARA's mission is to ensure ready access to essential evidence that documents the rights of American citizens, the actions of federal officials, and the national experience."

National Technical Information Service

www.ntis.gov/

This agency from the Commerce Department can help you search for government reports.

Project VoteSmart

www.vote-smart.org/

Explore this page for the types of information that you can learn about your congressional representative or senators.

USA Services

www.info.gov

This is an official government website that links citizens to the agencies of the federal government.

THOMAS, Legislative Information on the Internet

http://thomas.loc.gov/

Library of Congress site for learning about Congress and government. You can research current legislation and the *Congressional Record* since 1993. To go directly to the *Congressional Record* use **http:// thomas.loc.gov/home/legbranch/otherleg.html.**

U.S. Government Printing Office

http://www.gpo.gov/

The GPO is an arm of the Congress, and it is the largest publisher in the world. This site allows you to access its catalog. It does not link you to the sources themselves, however.

GPO Access

www.gpoaccess.gov

You can obtain access to many of the government documents through this website.

U.S. National Library of Medicine

http://www.nlm.nih.gov/

Use this for free medline searches and for finding reliable information on health related topics.

World-Wide Web Virtual Library of U.S. Government Information Sources

http://www.nttc.edu/resources/government/
govresources.asp

This site is maintained by the National Technology Transfer Center. It links you to numerous federal agencies and government commissions.

Find State and Local Government Agencies

State and Local Governments on the Net

http://www.statelocalgov.net/

Search this site to find servers for each of the fifty states. On each page, you will also find links to various branches of the state government, agencies, and county or city servers on the Internet.

Find Legal and Judicial Sources

FindLaw

http://www.findlaw.com/

Do topical search with a broad range of types of issues and court decisions.

Internet Legal Research Group

www.ilrg.com

This is a categorized index of more than 4,000 select websites and locally stored web pages, legal forms, and downloadable files. This site provides a comprehensive resource of the information available on the Internet concerning law and the legal profession, with an emphasis on the United States of America.

U.S. Department of Justice Search

`http://www.usdoj.gov/`

Use this page to find crime statistics and legal matters.

Find Multimedia and Internet Materials

The Chronology of New Media

`www.metromemetics.com/thechronology/`

This site includes a chronology of "New Media" beginning in China in the year 3,000 B.C.

Multimedia Directory

`www.scala.com/multimedia`

This is one of the largest and most complete multimedia directories on the Internet. It was originally built and maintained by the German National Research Center for Information Technology.

Download Software

`www.tucows.com`

Tucows is the original software download site. It currently provides acces to over 40,000 sorfware programs on a "freeware" or "shareware" basis. In addtion to standalone programs the software available can be used to enhance other programs.

Encyclopedias and Reference Sources

ENCYCLOPEDIAS

Encyclopedia Britannica

`http://www.britannica.com/`

This page provides information about the online version of the *Encyclopedia Britannica*. Access to its contents is free, but "subscribers get more."

Wikipedia

www.wikipedia.com

Wikipedia is discussed earlier in this section. It is worth a second visit.

The Encyclopedia Mythica

www.pantheon.org/

This collection of links about myth, legends and folklore includes hypertext for some of its entries.

DICTIONARIES AND GLOSSARIES

The Acronym Finder

www.acronymfinder.com

Type in an acronym and this site will search its collection of 75,000 to find a match.

American Heritage Dictionary

www.bartleby.com/61/

Look up words and their pronunciations.

Animated American Sign Language Dictionary

http://www.commtechlab.msu.edu/sites/aslweb/browser.htm

See and understand sign communications.

Brewer's Dictionary of Phrase and Fable

www.bartleby.com/81

Popular in hardcover since 1879, there is now a hypertext version. Use the alphabetic method of browsing or go to the main Bibliomania page to search at **http://www.bibliomania.com.**

The CMU Pronouncing Dictionary

www.speech.cs.cmu.edu/cgi-bin/cmudict/

Developed at Carnegie Mellon, this is a pronouncing dictionary that uses a system of phonetic markings.

The Ruth H. Hooker Research Library and Technical Information Center

`library.nrl.navy.mil`

This site is maintained by the Naval research Library. It provides a number of resources via a host of reference tools, includes links to writing assistance and style guides.

Life Science Dictionary

`http://biotech.icmb.utexas.edu/`

Developed by BioTech, you can use this to define terms in various fields of biology, chemistry, ecology, medicine, pharmacology, and toxicology. Take the "Guided Tour."

OneLook Dictionaries

`http://www.onelook.com/`

This dictionary includes a search tool, as well as categories in computers, technology, business, science, medicine, religion, sports and just about anything else.

A Dictionary of Scientific Quotations

`http://naturalscience.com/dsqhome.html/`

Quotes from famous scientists in the natural sciences, social sciences, environmental studies, and technology.

A Semantic Rhyming Dictionary

`http://www.rhymezone.com`

Type in a search word and you can see if there is a perfect match, a syllable rhyme or a homophone. Sounds like?

WWWebster Dictionary:

`www.m-w.com`

This is the online version of the Merriam Webster dictionary. You can search for phrases as well as words.

The WorldWideWeb Acronym and Abbreviation Server

`http://silmaril.ie/cgi-bin/uncgi/acronyms`

In addition to finding the meaning of an acronym, this database allows you to type in words to determine if they are included in an acronym.

What is

`http://whatis.com/`

Handy reference for speaking the language of computer geeks. You can scroll through a top frame of alphabetic terms or search.

Writing Tools

Bartlett's Familiar Quotations

`http://www.bartleby.com/#quotations`

Need a quote for your speech? Get it online from this classic source.

Garbl's Writing Resources On Line

`http://garbl.home.comcast.net/`

This site has many links to help the user write the perfect paper. These links are split into: English grammar, style, usage, plain language, 20 words, reference sources, online writing experts, word play and books on writing.

The Purdue University Writing Lab

`http://owl.english.purdue.edu/`

Useful source for writing tools.

Rôget's Thesaurus

`http://humanities.uchicago.edu/forms_unrest/`
`ROGET.html`

This is the 1911 edition, but still useful to find the synonym you need.

Strunk & White: The Elements of Style

`http://www.bartleby.com/141/index.html`

Got a grammatical question or concern about written form? You can find the answer here.

Newspapers

The Chicago Tribune

http://www.chicago.tribune.com/

This is the interactive edition for news from Chicago.

The Christian Science e-Monitor

http://www.csmonitor.com/

Using the site's express navigation tools, you can explore the wealth of features on the e-Monitor. The Monitor also enables you to search its archive for issues as far back as 1980.

The Los Angeles Times

http://www.latimes.com/

News from the West coast.

The New York Times

http://www.nytimes.com/

Premier national newspaper; "all the news that's fit to print" online.

Philadelphia Online

http://www.philly.com/

You can select online versions of the Philadelphia Inquirer or the Philadelphia Daily News.

Regional Newspapers

www.mcclatchy.com

This is the corporate site for the McClatchy Newspapers. McClatchy owns 32 major regional daily newspapers in fast growing cities around the U.S., as well as dozens of non-daily papers in other markets. Roll your mouse over the tabs at the top to see the newspapers and other periodicals.

USA Today

http://www.usatoday.com/

Daily national newspaper, and like its print counterpart, the online version is heavy on graphics and color, and light on the news.

Village Voice Worldwide

`www.villagevoice.com/`

Published weekly, this online version has the same social commentary and pop culture features as the tabloid version. Want to rent an apartment in SOHO?

Wall Street Journal

`www.wsj.com/`

This online version requires a subscription. You may do a two-week free trial subscription.

The Washington Post

`www.washingtonpost.com/`

Read the online version of the premier Washington daily. The online Post allows you to jump to sections with its keyword search.

Wire Services

The Associated Press

`http://www.newsday.com/news/nationworld/nation/wire`

This link from newsday.com allows you to access the Associated Press.

Online Magazines

Atlantic Monthly

`http://www.theatlantic.com/atlantic/`

The online version is called Atlantic Unbound. Click on the left side of the screen to access complete texts and an interactive forum.

CNN.com

`www.cnn.com`

See the online version of the original 24-hour cable news network. View the news by browsing the news categories or using the search tools.

The Economist

www.economist.com/

British magazine for discussion of a broad range of international topics.

Forbes Magazine

www.forbes.com/

Economic news from a business perspective from the digital "capitalist tool."

Foreign Affairs

www.foreignaffairs.org/

Prestigious journal for international policy.

Wired Magazine

www.wired.com

Wired Magazine proclaims its role to be one of "defining the web." This online version of the magazine allows browsing by category as well as searching.

Intellectual Capital.com

http://www.speakout.com/activism/opinions

This online publication features weekly topics on a range of social issues that would be very effective for persuasive speeches.

National Geographic

http://www.nationalgeographic.com/

Includes excellent multimedia tours featuring graphics, as well as audio and video.

The Nation

http://www.thenation.com/

Digital version of a traditional political magazine. A special feature is its link to multiple blogs—see right side.

National Review

http://www.nationalreview.com/

Conservative journal on political issues, published by William F. Buckley. Includes multiple ways to browse and search.

The New Republic

www.tnr.com

Journal of opinion emphasizing current political topics, offering a range of ideological perspectives from liberal to neo-conservative. The online version provides a sample of the articles in the full hard-copy edition.

Policy Review

http://www.heritage.org/policyreview

News and political magazine from the conservative point of view of the Heritage Foundation.

Scientific American

http://www.sciam.com/index.html/

This is the home page for *Scientific American.*

Salon Magazine

http://www.salon.com/

Find materials on popular culture and social trends in this magazine. NOTE: You must view an advertisement to avoid paying for access.

Slate

www.slate.com

Online news magazine created by Microsoft, solely as an Internet political and social policy magazine.

Time Magazine

www.time.com

View the major sections of the newsweekly and follow links to current issues as well as past issues.

US News and World Report

www.usnews.com

The publisher of a leading newsweekly and a leading guide to college rankings makes its news material available online.

Broadcast News Networks

ABC

www.abcnews.com

The page from ABC offers links to the various national news programs on the network.

CNBC—The Leader in Business News

http://moneycentral.msn.com/home.asp

This is the home page for MSN Money and CNBC, a leader in business news. This site offers a business center, media clips, and a schedule of daytime and primetime guests. The user can also link to CNBC Business videos from this site.

CNN Interactive

http://cnn.com/

Be sure to scroll down to browse the range of topics and discussion areas available from CNN.

FOX NEWS

http://foxnews.com/

From the FOX you can read headlines and link to some of its news programs.

C-SPAN—Your Online Resource for Public Affairs

http://www.c-span.org/

C-SPAN's home page provides the user with audio and video footage, a schedule of today's happenings in Congress, a search engine, C-SPAN in the classroom, and allows the user to shop for videos and other products.

MSNBC

http://www.msnbc.com

Find stories that were broadcast on the NBC network as well as on its cable affiliate, MSNBC.

PBS

http://www.pbs.org/

The Public Broadcasting System is online. Many PBS programs provide a wealth of online information in conjunction notes about the programs themselves.

Legislative

The Federal News Service

http://www.fnsg.com/

This is a source used by journalists to find transcripts of Congressional hearings and to find statements made by national and international leaders. It is a commercial site, and thus some of its features are for subscribers only. But the free parts are worthwhile.

U.S. House of Representatives

http://www.house.gov/

House home page provides links to information about the legislative process, bills under deliberation and a directory for House members. The page also provides links to other government sources.

U.S. Senate

http://www.senate.gov/

Find the address for your senator. There is also a useful guide to Senate committees.

CWA Political/Legislative Web

http://www.cwa-union.org/

"The Communications Workers of America Web site provides the user with hot issues about federal agencies, specific state issues, a link to CWA political/legislative department, CWA Bill of Rights, and the option to write to your congressperson."

Library of Congress

www.loc.gov/

Library of Congress offers information in history, an exhibitions gallery, current events, legislative information, details on catalogs, collections and research references and a special bicentennial birthday page.

Statistical Abstracts from the U.S. Census Bureau

www.census.gov/

Information you can search from the last census.

Federal Bureau of Investigation

http://www.fbi.gov/

The FBI's home page includes: community outreach programs, FBI academy information, FAQs, contacting different offices, history of the FBI, 90th anniversary ceremony, and tour information. Also included is a kid's page.

The White House

www.whitehouse.gov/

Send email to the president or vice president. You can also tap into various units of the Executive branch. Search the archives for past presidential statements and RealAudio files of presidential speeches.

Judicial

Court TV Law Center

http://www.courttv.com/

Links from this page direct you to resources for some of the most popular cases that have been aired on this cable TV program from its case files. There are less notorious cases as well. Of special use for giving a persuasive speech are the sections on elder law and family law. Click on each to find a list of topics and brief background about some issues. To browse for topics, go to **http://www. courttv.com/lawlinks/** for an alphabetic listing of cases in its lawlinks.

CyberSpace Law Center

www.findlaw.com

This is an excellent source if you are looking for a topic dealing with legal issues surrounding the Internet.

Federal Courts Finder

http://www.law.emory.edu/FEDCTS/

Use this site to locate decisions from circuit courts around the country.

National Criminal Justice Reference Service

www.ncjrs.gov

NCJRS is a federally funded resource administered by the Department of Justice. It offers justice and substance abuse information to support research, policy, and program development.

National Institute of Justice

http://www.ojp.usdoj.gov/nij/

This is an agency of the Department of Justice that does research and makes recommendations on policies for dealing with crime problems.

Uniform Crime Reports

http://fisher.lib.virginia.edu/crime

Use the University of Virginia Social Sciences Library to look up statistics on types of crime. The UVA Library uses FBI crime statistics. You can sort by types of crime and a geographic reporting unit. Follow the directions for making your selections and the form of the output of the data.

United States Department of Justice

www.usdoj.gov/

This cabinet agency of the federal government bills itself as the "largest law firm in the Nation."

WWW Virtual Law Library

www.law.indiana.edu/v-lib/

Go to the Indiana University location for this data base to use for legal research. It also has a link to numerous search tools dealing with law.

LEGAL DICTIONARIES

Court TV Glossary of Legal Terms

www.courttv.com/legalterms/glossary.html/

Alphabetic listings of legal terms.

Library of Congress Thesauri

www.loc.gov/lexico/servlet/lexico

This site houses links to several vocabulary lists maintained by the Library of Congress. Notable are the ones dealing with legal information and legislative terminology. It is often very useful to explore a thesaurus when seeking synonyms for refining your research.

WWWLIA Legal Dictionary

www.dvhaime.org/dictionary

You can find terms from American law, or for other English speaking countries with a legal system based in Anglo-Saxon common law.

Sources for Audience Analysis

DEMOGRAPHIC STUDIES

Bureau of Labor Statistics

http://stats.bls.gov//

Use this source to find socioeconomic data.

Center for Demography and Ecology

http://www.ssc.wisc.edu/cde/

The University of Wisconsin at Madison's Center for Demography and Ecology includes information on demography from training seminar schedules to online publications.

Social Science Research Computing Center

http://www.spc.uchicago.edu/DATALIB/

The SSRC at the University of Chicago has collected links dealing with demography and census data. Click on "data holdings" to browse or do a keyword search.

United Nations Scholars' Workstation

www.library.yale.edu/un

Yale University maintains the United Nations Scholars' Workstation as a resource containing texts, finding aids, data sets, maps, and pointers to print and electronic information. Subject coverage includes disarmament, economic and social development, environment, human rights, international relations, international trade, peacekeeping, and population and demography.

World Wide Web Virtual Library Demography and Population Studies

http://demography.anu.edu.au/VirtualLibrary/

This is a mammoth list of links to places around the globe on various facets of demography. It is maintained by the Australian National University.

University of Virginia Social Sciences Data Center County and City Data

http://fisher.lib.virginia.edu/ccdb

This is a handy interactive page for finding demographic data for many cities in the country. The County and City Books are based principally on U.S. Census data.

U.S. Census Bureau

http://www.census.gov/

Find reports from the last census as well as frequent updates on the U.S. population and economic indicators. The page offers a variety of tools for accessing demographic data. A particularly useful tool for learning census information about a particular community is found at the U.S. Gazetteer link. Go to **http://www.census.gov/cgi-bin/gazetteer/.** You can use this page to search for demographic data by zip code.

PSYCHOGRAPHICS

Population Reference Bureau

www.prb.org

This is a population information resource. This site offers a comprehensive directory of population related Web sites, available by keyword search, topic, and region.

United Nations Population Information Network (POPIN)

http://www.un.org/popin

This site offers information on the trends of world population and regional population.

Internet Domain Survey

http://www.isc.org/ds/

This is a demographic page for the World Wide Web. Statistics, including number of hosts, on the Web are available as well as past survey results and related links.

PUBLIC OPINION STUDIES

The Gallup Organization

http://www.gallup.com/

This is the home page for Gallup. On it you will find links to a few of its most recent studies on national opinions. Harris Polls: (See Institute for Research in Social Science Public below).

The General Social Survey

http://www.icpsr.umich.edu/gss/

Use the omnibus personal interview of U.S. households done by the National Opinion Research Center to find attitudes on a variety of social issues. The Subject Index provides an alphabetic listing by topics. Use the GSS Module Index to see batteries of questions on themes.

The National Election Studies Guide to Public Opinion and Electoral Behavior

http://www.umich.edu/~nes/nesguide/nesguide.htm

The National Election Studies (NES) is affiliated with the University of Michigan Institute for Social Research. This page provides data about religious affiliation, ideological identification, and results of opinion iresearch on a wide range of social and political topics.

Yankelovich

`http://www.yankelovich.com/`

Use this site to learn about studies conducted by Yankelovich. There are descriptions of a few studies, but to access the entirety of each report, you need to purchase Yankelovich reports; however, a 30-day free access trial is available.

Multimedia

Adobe Systems

`http://www.adobe.com/`

Adobe's Photoshop is the standard in the field. Another useful product is Adobe's PDF, (Portable Document Format) for converting a variety of types of multimedia file formats for use on HTML pages.

HTML Code Tutorial

`www.htmlcodetutorial.com`

If you want to develop a web page for yourself, you really need to learn some HyperText Markup Language (HTML) An elegant tutorial for learning HTML lives at this site.

The Bare Bones Guide to HTML

`http://werbach.com/barebones/`

This is an online guide to coding HTML specifications. It also explains Netscape extensions.

HTML Goodies

`http://www.htmlgoodies.com/`

This compendium of resources for developing Web pages was created by Dr. Joe Burns. You can find free art work and scripts for your Web page.

PowerPoint Tutorial

`http://einstein.cs.uri.edu/tutorials/csc101/`
`powerpoint/ppt.html`

This site provides a comprehensive yet easy to follow tutorial for using PowerPoint.

Microsoft Downloads

`http://www.microsoft.com/msdownload/`

For users of Windows, this is a great source for downloading free software. A number of multimedia tools used for Web viewing are available, including the Microsoft Internet Explorer, the PowerPoint Animation viewer, the PowerPoint Viewer, ActiveX Controls, Microsoft's VRML Viewer, and Web authoring tools that work with the various components of the Microsoft Office. This page also links you to product information about PowerPoint, the component of the Microsoft Office most useful to public speakers for creating presentations.

COREL

`www.corel.com`

COREL is the producer of Paint Shop Pro, one of the most versatile graphics programs for manipulating bitmap images.

Netscape

`browser.netscape.com`

Download the latest version of this popular browser. Also link to information about internet security and obtain spyware and adware protection.

Marke Pesce—Outside the Light-Cone

`http://hyperreal.org/~mpesce`

Pesce is a pioneer in developing virtual reality. This is his Web page with links to the various papers that he has presented.

RealNetworks—The Home of RealAudio

`http://www.real.com/`

Go here to download a copy of the RealPlayer for receiving streamed audio and video in RealAudio and RealVideo formats.

WebMonkey

`www.webmonkey.com`

This is a good place to start if you are just beginning to learn about the web. It is also a good resource for these more experienced who really want to explore its power. Links at top right direct the beginner, builder or master to the appropriate information.

Audio and Video

C-SPAN Online

http://www.c-span.org/

Listen to sessions of the House and Senate and find a directory of what is going on on the Hill.

FedNet

http://www.fednet.net/

You can listen to audio and watch video coverage of select House and Senate committee hearings as well as floor action from Congress at this site. FedNet also maintains past files.

U.S. Department of Defense Live News Briefings

http://www.defenselink.mil/briefings/

This site provides live news briefings pertaining to Department of Defense. There are also text archives of past months' and years' briefings.

Sites and Sounds from ABC

http://www.abcnews.go.com/video/playerindex

This page offers news reports and commentary on the day's news.

Historical Archives

American Memory Collection

www.memory.loc.gov/ammem

The Library of Congress maintains a free Internet site of written and spoken words, sound recordings, still and moving images, prints, maps, and sheet music that document the American experience. It is a digital record of American history and creativity. These materials, from the collections of the Library of Congress and other institutions, chronicle historical events, people, places, and ideas that continue to shape America, serving the public as a resource for education and lifelong learning. You can browse by topic, search or "Ask a Librarian."

American Rhetoric Project

www.americanrhetoric.com

This site contains text and audio of speeches delivered in a number of settings and venues. It also includes links to the study of rhetoric and to speeches that can be found in the movies.

Biography.com

http://www.biography.com/

Search this database of famous people to learn how every life has a story.

National Archives

www.archives.gov

The National Archives is the federal repository of documents and materials created in the course of business conducted by the United States Federal government. While only a small fraction of the documents so created are so important that they are kept forever, the Archive still is a vast repository. Through this site, you can browse and search much of the material that might relate to a research assignment. See the links on the left for the gateway to historical documents and the presidential libraries.

History Channel

http://www.historychannel.com/

Equipped with a "This Day in History" feature, this site offers the user many options. The user can search, take a history quiz, vote in a poll, and browse general history news.

Inaugural Addresses of U.S. Presidents

http://www.bartleby.com/124/index.html

This collection from Columbia University links you to each of the Presidential Inauguration Addresses from George Washington to George W. Bush.

White House Audio Archive

http://www.whitehouse.gov/radio/

Go to this page to listen to Saturday Radio Addresses presented by President Bush. The page includes a search engine that you can use to find a speech by topic area or date.

Supreme Court Multimedia

`www.oyez.org`

The OYEZ Project provides access to more than 2000 hours of Supreme Court audio. All audio in the Court recorded since 1995 is included in the project. Before 1995, the audio collection is selective. The database can be browsed and searched. News of the course is also included.

WebCorp Historical Speeches Archive

`http://www.webcorp.com/sounds/`

Sound bites from speeches since the 1930s on a variety of topics. There is also a video collection from the Nixon era and the Watergate scandal. Some sound offerings are available in RealAudio.

News Archives

Back in Time

`www.time.com`

Search stories that appeared in time magazine back to the 1920s. Access to all articles requires a subscription; however, a wealth of information is available without fee.

CNN Interactive Video Vault

`www.cnn.com/video_vault/index.html/`

Apple QuickTime movies and video clips using the VIVO format are featured. You can find highlights from the latest stories carried on CNN as well as clips from stories from the past three years.

Vanderbilt News Archive

`http://tvnews.vanderbilt.edu`

The Television News Archive collection at Vanderbilt University is the world's most available, extensive and complete archive of television news. Since 1968, the Archive has consistently recorded, indexed, and preserved network television news for research, review, and study. You will need to register, but this is free. Video tapes of archived news shows may be requested, you pay for the cost of duplication and shipping.

Other Online Resources

Allyn & Bacon Public Speaking Web Site

www.abacon.com/pubspeak/

This Web site contains six modules you can use along with your public speaking text to learn about the process of public speaking and help prepare for speeches.

The site focuses on the five steps of speech preparation: Assessing Your Speechmaking Situation, Analyzing Your Audience, Researching Your Topic, Organizing and Writing Your Speech, Delivering Your Presentation, and Discerning Other Talks.

Special Features:
- Interactive activities aid in speech preparation.
- "Notes from the Instructor" provide additional details on selected topics
- Web links throughout are updated regularly and allow you to use and explore reliable Internet sites related to public speaking

Allyn & Bacon Communication Studies Site

www.abacon.com/commstudies

Learn more about the process of communication! The topics of Small Group Communication, Interpersonal Communication and Public Speaking all are covered in depth. Each module includes notes, interactive exercises, and quizzes. A special "Teaching Resources"section includes sample syllabi, a listing of professional resources, and more.

NOTES

NOTES

NOTES

NOTES

NOTES

NOTES

NOTES

NOTES

NOTES

NOTES